THE ESSENCE OF TIBETAN BUDDHISM

MAY THE BUDDHADHARMA REACH ALL SENTIENT BEINGS · LAMA YESHE WISDOM ARCHIVE ·

Previously published by the LAMA YESHE WISDOM ARCHIVE

Becoming Your Own Therapist, by Lama Yeshe
Advice for Monks and Nuns, by Lama Yeshe and Lama Zopa Rinpoche
Virtue and Reality, by Lama Zopa Rinpoche
Make Your Mind an Ocean, by Lama Yeshe
Teachings from the Vajrasattva Retreat, by Lama Zopa Rinpoche
Daily Purification: A Short Vajrasattva Practice, by Lama Zopa Rinpoche
The Essence of Tibetan Buddhism, by Lama Yeshe
Making Life Meaningful, by Lama Zopa Rinpoche
Teachings from the Mani Retreat, by Lama Zopa Rinpoche
Direct and Unmistaken Method, by Lama Zopa Rinpoche
The Yoga of Offering Food, by Lama Zopa Rinpoche

For initiates only:

A Chat about Heruka, by Lama Zopa Rinpoche
A Chat about Yamantaka, by Lama Zopa Rinpoche

In association with TDL Publications, Los Angeles:

Mirror of Wisdom, by Geshe Tsultim Gyeltsen
Illuminating the Path, by His Holiness the Dalai Lama

May whoever sees, touches, reads, remembers, or talks or thinks about these books never be reborn in unfortunate circumstances, receive only rebirths in situations conducive to the perfect practice of Dharma, meet only perfectly qualified spiritual guides, quickly develop bodhicitta and immediately attain enlightenment for the sake of all sentient beings.

LAMA YESHE

THE ESSENCE OF TIBETAN BUDDHISM
The Three Principal Aspects of the Path and
Introduction to Tantra

Edited by Nicholas Ribush

LAMA YESHE WISDOM ARCHIVE • BOSTON
www.LamaYeshe.com
A non-profit charitable organization for the benefit of
all sentient beings and a section of the Foundation for the
Preservation of the Mahayana Tradition
www.fpmt.org

First published 2001
15,000 copies for free distribution
Second printing 2003, 15,000

LAMA YESHE WISDOM ARCHIVE
PO BOX 356
WESTON
MA 02493 USA

ISBN 1-891868-08-X

10 9 8 7 6 5 4 3 2

Front cover, photographer unknown
Designed by Mark Gatter

Please contact the LAMA YESHE WISDOM ARCHIVE for more free
copies of this book

CONTENTS

BENEFACTORS' DEDICATIONS

I dedicate this book to my father and mother, Gene and Verdena Orrico. Thank you both for instilling in me integrity, a sense of humor and the never-ending gift of love.

I would also like to thank my husband's parents, Alice and Robert Harper, now deceased but ever in our hearts. If not for them we would not have been able to give as much as we have toward helping others. I rejoice in their merit!

And to our dear, deceased friend, John Marvin Schwartz, who touched countless lives. May his undying words continue to influence and reach out to all hearts: "Hey, we are still alive, with another chance to make a difference in the world!"

Dedicated with love,
Mary Harper

With deepest gratitude to my teachers, past and present—including His Holiness the Dalai Lama, Kyabje Zong Rinpoche, Lama Yeshe, Lama Zopa Rinpoche and Geshe Gyeltsen—I dedicate all merit to their long lives, the spread of the holy Dharma throughout the ten directions and the enlightenment of all sentient beings.

I also thank my Dharma friends, who have been so helpful in my practice—especially the kind John Allen, who has always given most generously—and the Lama Yeshe Wisdom Archive, for the opportunity to create great merit in this way.

Doren Harper

PUBLISHER'S ACKNOWLEDGMENTS

We are extremely grateful to our friends and supporters who have made it possible for the LAMA YESHE WISDOM ARCHIVE to both exist and function: to Lama Yeshe and Lama Zopa Rinpoche, whose kindness is impossible to repay; to Peter and Nicole Kedge and Venerable Ailsa Cameron for helping bring the ARCHIVE to its present state of development; to Venerable Roger Kunsang, Lama Zopa's tireless assistant, for his kindness and consideration; and to our sustaining supporters: Drs. Penny Noyce & Leo Liu, Barry & Connie Hershey, Joan Terry, Roger & Claire Ash-Wheeler, Claire Atkins, Tom & Suzanne Castles, Hawk Furman, Richard Gere, Lily Chang Wu and Thubten Yeshe.

In particular, we would like to thank Doren & Mary Harper, who have been such a great support to the LAMA YESHE WISDOM ARCHIVE as well as many other Dharma projects over three decades, especially Thubten Dhargye Ling, Long Beach, California, for their kind sponsorship of the reprint of this book.

We are also deeply grateful to those who have also been major contributors or book sponsors over the past few years: Dean Alper, Paula Antony, Christine Arlington, Peggy Bennington, Dharmawati Brechbuhl, Ross Brooke, Rose Canfield, the Caytons (Lori, Karuna, Pam, Bob & Amy), Lai-Hing Chong, Ngawang Chotak, Kok Leng Chuah, John Clulow, Denise Dagley, Paula de Wijs-Koolkin, Chris Dornan, Cecily Drucker, Derek & Soon Hui Goh, Dan & Tara Bennett Goleman, Lorraine Greenfield, Richard F. Hay, Heruka Center, Wendy Hobbs, Su Hung, Ecie Hursthouse, Barbara Jenson, Kadampa Center, Bill Kelly & Robyn Brentano, Eric Klaft, Tony LaGreca, Land of Medicine Buddha, Chiu-Nan Lai, Chiu-Mei Lai, Henry & Catherine Lau, Salim Lee, Harry Leong (in loving memory of his father, Woon Leong), Mony & Ester Liberman, SS Lim, Judy Mindrol Lin, Jamieson Lowe, Sandra Magnussen, Doss McDavid, Kathleen McDonald, Ellen McInerney, Amy McKhann, Petra McWilliams, Tara Melwani, Therese Miller, Lynda Millspaugh, Ueli Minder, Janet Moore, Jack Morison, Esther Ngai, Trong Nguyen, Gerard O'Halloran,

Dennis Paulson, James Pelkey, Leslie Reincke, Dorian Ribush, Rev. Janyce Riedel, Claire Ritter, Ven. Ingeborg Sandberg, Mayra Rocha Sandoval, Jesse Sartain, Jack Sonnabaum & Judith Hunt, Datuk Tai Tsu Kuang, Tan Swee Eng, Tom Thorning, Thubten Norbu Ling Center, Tushita Retreat Centre, Wendy van den Heuvel, Diana van Die (in loving memory of Lenie van Die), Oanh Vovan, Tom Waggoner & Renee Robison, Vajrapani Institute, Robbie Watkins and Wisdom Publications.

We would like, as well, to express our appreciation for the kindness and compassion of all those other generous benefactors mentioned in detail in our previous publications and those who have contributed funds to our work since our last published list a couple of years ago. They are too numerous to mention individually in this book, but we value highly each and every donation made to spreading the Dharma for the sake of the kind mother sentient beings and now pay tribute to you all on our Web site, www.LamaYeshe.com. Thank you so much.

I would also like to pay tribute to our dear and long-time friend and supporter who helped us and many other Dharma and Tibet-related projects for almost thirty years, Carol Davies, who passed away in Perth earlier this year, far too soon. May she and all other sentient beings immediately realize bodhicitta and quickly attain supreme enlightenment.

I also thank the many kind people who have asked that their donations be kept anonymous; the volunteers who have given so generously of their time to help us with our mailings, especially Therese Miller; my wife, Wendy Cook, for her tireless help and support; our dedicated office staff, Jennifer Barlow and Linda Merle; Alison Ribush & Mandala Books (Melbourne) and Veronica Kaczmarowski & FPMT Australia for much appreciated assistance with our work in Australia; and Dennis Heslop, Philip Bradley and our other friends at Wisdom Books (London) for their great help with our work in Europe. We appreciate, too, the kindness and expertise of our main volunteer transcribers, Su Hung, Segen Speer-Senner and Gareth Robinson. We also thank most sincerely Massimo Corona and the FPMT International Office for their generous financial and administrative assistance.

Finally, I want to express my gratitude to Greg Sneddon and his wonderful team of volunteers in Melbourne, Australia— including Dr. Su Hung, Anne Pottage, Llysse Valez, Chris Friedl and Anthony Deague—who recently completed digitizing almost our entire archive of more than 10,000 hours of teachings by Lama Yeshe and Lama Zopa Rinpoche and will continue to help us in this area.

Special gratitude is extended to the wonderful Mark Gatter for his invaluable help and fine esthetic in the design and production of this and most of our other books.

If you, dear reader, would like to join this noble group of open-hearted altruists by contributing to the production of more free books by Lama Yeshe or Lama Zopa Rinpoche or to any other aspect of the LAMA YESHE WISDOM ARCHIVE's work, please contact us to find out how.

—*Dr. Nicholas Ribush*

Through the merit of having contributed to the spread of the Buddha's teachings for the sake of all sentient beings, may our benefactors and their families and friends have long and healthy lives, all happiness, and may all their Dharma wishes be instantly fulfilled.

EDITOR'S INTRODUCTION

This publication is the third in our series of free books by Lama Yeshe, following the extremely popular and well received *Becoming Your Own Therapist* and *Make Your Mind an Ocean*.

It differs, however, in that the material contained herein is also on video, which we have put onto CD (plays only on computer; see the back pages of this book for details), so that you can now see and hear Lama Yeshe giving these teachings. Just like our books, the CDs are free. We have edited this book less intensively than normal so that the text quite closely adheres to Lama's original words and phraseology, making it easier to follow when watching the CDs. For the same reason, we have also left intact Lama's references to world events of the time, such as the various Middle East dramas of 1979–80.

Lama's teachings were dynamic events full of energy and laughter. He taught not only verbally but physically and facially as well. Thus, we encourage you to get the CDs of these teachings in order to get as total an experience of the incomparable Lama Yeshe as possible.

The first teaching, "The Three Principal Aspects of the Path," was given in France in 1982, during an FPMT-sponsored tour of Europe by His Holiness the Dalai Lama. Just before His Holiness's scheduled teachings at Institut Vajra Yogini, His Holiness manifested illness and asked Lama Yeshe to fill in for a couple of days—to "baby-sit" the audience, as Lama put it. This wonderful two-part teaching on the three principal aspects of the path is the result.

The second teaching, an "Introduction to Tantra," also in two parts, was given at Grizzly Lodge, California, in 1980. It comprises the first two lectures of a commentary on the Chenrezig yoga method taught by Lama at the request of Vajrapani Institute, Boulder Creek. The entire course was videotaped and we plan to make available the remaining six tapes as soon as we can enhance their sound and picture quality.

I am most grateful to Linda Gatter and Wendy Cook for their editorial input, which greatly enhanced the text of this book, and to Greg Sneddon and his team in Melbourne, Australia, who converted the videos of these teachings to CD in between digitizing all 10,000 or more hours of ARCHIVE audio! Thank you all so much for your help.

THE THREE PRINCIPAL ASPECTS
OF THE PATH

THE THREE PRINCIPAL ASPECTS
OF THE PATH

FIRST TEACHING: RENUNCIATION, BODHICITTA AND EMPTINESS

At Institut Vajra Yogini, France, during an FPMT-sponsored teaching tour of Europe in 1982, His Holiness the Dalai Lama manifested ill health and asked Lama Yeshe to fill in for him for the first day's teachings. The following teachings ensued.

Today, I'm unfortunate. And today, you're unfortunate as well, because you have to put up with me, the garbage man. You have to put up with my garbage; I'm the garbage man. Due to circumstance, His Holiness is experiencing some discomfort with his health, so we should all pray for his good health...and so that it won't be necessary to be in this situation, where you have to put up with my garbage. However, due to these circumstances, His Holiness has given me permission to baby-sit you.

Now, His Holiness has chosen a particular text by Lama Je Tsong Khapa, which we call *The Three Principal Paths to Liberation, or Enlightenment.* So today I'm going to try to give you an introduction to this text, but going into it in detail is not my business.

In Tibetan, we call this text *Lam-tso nam-sum.* Historically, this book derives from Lama Je Tsong Khapa's direct, visual communication with Lord Manjushri. Manjushri gave him this teaching and then Lama Je Tsong Khapa gave it to his disciples: *Lam-tso nam-sum*, the *Three Principal Aspects*. This is a small text, but it contains the essence of the entire teaching of Lord Buddha. Also, while it is very simple and practical, it is a universal teaching that everybody can understand.

Now, the three principles are renunciation, bodhicitta and the wisdom of shunyata; these three are called the principal, essential paths to liberation.

I want you to understand why they are called the three essential, or principal, paths to liberation, because in the Western world, the word "renunciation" has a different connotation; people get scared that they will lose their pleasure. But without renunciation, there's no way out.

RENUNCIATION

First of all, all of us consider that we would like to be free from ego mind and the bondage of samsara. But what binds us to samsara and makes us unhappy is not having renunciation. Now, what is renunciation? What makes us renounced?

The reason we are unhappy is because we have extreme craving for sense objects, samsaric objects, and we grasp at them. We are seeking to solve our problems but we are not seeking in the right place. The right place is our own ego grasping; we have to loosen that tightness, that's all.

According to the Buddhist point of view, monks and nuns

16

are supposed to hold renunciation vows. The meaning of monks and nuns renouncing the world is that they have less craving for and grasping at sense objects. But you cannot say that they have already given up samsara, because monks and nuns still have stomachs! The thing is that the English word "renounce" is linguistically tricky. You can say that monks and nuns renounce their stomachs, but that doesn't necessarily mean they actually throw their stomachs away.

So, I want you to understand that renouncing sensory pleasure doesn't mean throwing nice things away. Even if you do, it doesn't mean you have renounced them. Renunciation is a totally inner experience. Renunciation of samsara does not mean you throw samsara away because your body and your nose are samsara. How can you throw your nose away? Your mind and body are samsara —well, at least mine are. So I cannot throw them away. Therefore, renunciation means less craving; it means being more reasonable instead of putting too much psychological pressure on yourself and acting crazy.

The important point for us to know, then, is that we should have less grasping at sense pleasures, because most of the time our grasping at and craving desire for worldly pleasure does not give us satisfaction. That is the main point. It leads to more dissatisfaction and to psychologically crazier reactions. That is the main point.

If you have the wisdom and method to handle objects of the five senses perfectly such that they do not bring negative reactions, it's all right for you to touch them. And, as human beings, we should be capable of judging for ourselves how far we can go into the experience of sense pleasure without getting mixed up and confused. We should judge for ourselves; it is completely up to individual experience. It's like French wine—some people cannot take it at all. Even though they would like to, the constitution of their nervous system doesn't allow it. But other people can take a little; others can take a bit more; some can take a lot.

So, I want you to understand why Buddhist scriptures completely forbid monks and nuns from drinking wine. It is not because wine is bad; grapes are bad. Grapes and vines are beautiful; the color of red wine is fantastic. But because we are ordinary beginners on the path to liberation, we can easily get caught up in negative energy. That's the reason. It is not that wine itself is bad. This is a good example for renunciation.

Who was the great Indian saint who drank wine? Do you remember that story? I don't recall who it was, but this saint went into a bar and drank and drank until the bartender finally asked him, "How are you going to pay?" The saint replied, "I'll pay when the sun sets." But the sun didn't set and the saint just kept on drinking. The bartender wanted his money but somehow he controlled the sunset. These kinds of higher realization—we can call them miraculous or esoteric realizations—are beyond the comprehension of ordinary people like us, but this saint was able to control the sun and drank perhaps thirty gallons of wine. And he didn't even have to make pee-pee!

Now, my point is that renunciation of samsara is not only the business of monks and nuns. Whoever is seeking liberation or enlightenment needs renunciation of samsara. If you check your own life, your own daily experiences, you will see that you are caught up in small pleasures—we [Buddhists] consider such grasping to be a tremendous hang-up and not of much value. However, the Western way of thinking—"I should have the best; the biggest"—is similar to our Buddhist attitude that we should have the best, most lasting, perfect pleasure rather than spending our lives fighting for the pleasure of a glass of wine.

Therefore, the grasping attitude and useless actions have to be abandoned and things that make your life meaningful and liberated have to be actualized.

But I don't want you to understand only the philosophical point of view. We are capable of examining our own minds and comprehending what kind of mind brings everyday problems and is not worthwhile, both objectively and subjectively. This is the way that meditation allows us to correct our attitudes and actions. Don't think, "My attitudes and actions come from my previous karma, therefore I can't do anything." That's a misunderstanding of karma. Don't think, "I am powerless." Human beings do have power. We have the power to change our lifestyles, change our attitudes, change our habits. We can call that capacity Buddha potential, God potential or whatever you want to call it. That's why Buddhism is simple. It is a universal teaching that can be understood by all people, religious or non-religious.

The opposite of renunciation of samsara—to put what I'm saying another way—is the extreme mind that we have most of the time: the grasping, craving mind that gives us an overestimated projection of objects, which has nothing to with the reality of those objects.

However, I want you to understand that Buddhism is not saying that objects have no beauty whatsoever. They do have beauty—a flower has a certain beauty, but that beauty is only conventional, or relative. The craving mind, however, projects onto an object something that is beyond the relative level, which has nothing to do with that object, that hypnotizes us. That mind is hallucinating, deluded and holding the wrong entity.

Without intensive observation or introspective wisdom, we cannot discover this. For that reason, Buddhist meditation includes checking. We call checking in this way analytical meditation. It involves logic; it involves philosophy. So Buddhist philosophy and psychology help us see things better. Therefore, analytical meditation is a scientific way of analyzing our own experience.

Finally, I also want you to understand that monks and nuns may not be renounced at all. It's true, isn't it? In Buddhism, we talk about superficial structure and universal structure. So when we say monks and nuns renounce, it means we're trying, that's all. Westerners sometimes think monks and nuns are holy. We're not holy; we're just trying. That's reasonable. Don't overestimate again, on that. Lay people, monks and nuns—we're all members of the Buddhist community. We should understand each other well and then let go; leave things as they are. It's unhealthy to have overestimated expectations of each other.

OK, now I'd better get back to business. I think that's enough of an introduction to renunciation. Now, bodhicitta.

BODHICITTA

Bodhicitta is like this. First, you have to understand your own ego problems—craving, desire, anger, impatience; your own situation, your inability to cope, your own disasters—within yourself and feel compassion for yourself. Because of the situation you're in, start by becoming the object of your own compassion. It begins from there: "This situation I'm in, I'm not the only one with ego conflict and problems. In all the world's societies, some people are upper class, some middle and others low; some are extremely beautiful, some are medium and others are ugly. But, just like me, everybody seeks happiness and does not desire to be miserable."

In this way, a feeling of equilibrium begins to come. Somehow, deep within you, equilibrium towards enemies, strangers and friends arises—it is not merely intellectual but something really sincere. It comes from deep down; from the bottom of your heart.

Buddhism teaches you the meditational technique for equalizing all living beings in the universe. Without a certain degree of equilibrium feeling with all universal living beings, it's impossible to say, "I want to give my life to others." Nor is it possible to develop bodhicitta. Bodhicitta is most precious, a diamond mind. In order to have space for bodhicitta, you have to feel that all universal living beings are equal.

But I want you to understand the distinction between the communist and the Buddhist idea of equality. It's possible for you to experience the Buddhist idea of equilibrium right now; you can't experience the communist idea even after a billion years—unless everybody has a gun! It's not possible.

The point is that Buddhism considers that we should have realization of equilibrium because we need a healthy mind. Equalizing others is something to be done within my mind, not by changing human beings externally. My business is not to be bothered by mental projections of disliked enemy, grasped-at friend or forgettable stranger. These three categories of object are made by my own mind; they do not exist outside.

As long as you have as an object of hatred even one human being, as long as you have an overestimated object of craving desire, as long as you have an indifferent object of ignorance—someone you ignore and don't care about—as long as you have the three poisons of hatred, desire and ignorance in relation to these three objects, *you* have a problem. It is not the objects' problem.

How can I be happy if Elisabeth [the French interpreter] is my biggest problem, my enemy? How can I be happy? Equilibrium is something to do with the inner experience. Forget about bodhicitta—we all have a long way to go. What I'm trying to express is that Tibetan Buddhism and Lama Tsong Khapa consider that equilibrium is most difficult to realize. So, it's worthwhile at least to try. Even though it is difficult, try.

Another way of describing equilibrium is to call it the middle way. That is why, from a practical point of view, in order for Buddhists to be healthy we should have an equalized feeling with Western religion and eastern religion. We should have an equalized feeling and respect for people who practice Christianity. That's the way to be happy, and happiness is your main business. I think it's a mistake for Western baby Buddhists to think that Buddhism is better than Christianity. It's wrong. First of all, it's not true, and secondly, it creates bad vibrations and makes your mind unhealthy.

I really feel that Buddhists can learn a lot from Christians. Recently I was in Spain and visited some Christian monasteries. The renunciation and way of life of some of those Christian monks seems much better than the renunciation I've seen in many Tibetan monasteries. Monks in Tibetan monastic communities often have individualistic attitudes, whereas the monks I saw in the Christian communities seemed to be completely unified. They had no individual possessions. For me, those monks were objects of refuge. Of course, if being individualistic is what an individual needs for his or her spiritual growth, that's all right. That's why different religions exist.

However, you should practice equilibrium in your daily life as much as you can. Try to have neither enemies nor objects of tremendous, exaggerated grasping. In this way, in the space of your equilibrium, you can grow bodhicitta—the attitude dedicated to all universal living beings.

Bodhicitta is an extremely high realization. It is the complete opposite of the self-cherishing attitude. You completely give yourself into the service of others in order to lead them to the highest liberation, which is beyond temporary happiness.

Our thoughts are extreme. Sometimes we put too much emphasis on and tremendous energy into activities from which we gain nothing. Look at certain athletes, for example; or people who put all their money and energy into motorcycle jumping and end up killing themselves. What for?

Bodhicitta is very practical, I tell you. It's like medicine. The self-cherishing thought is like a nail or a sword in your heart; it always feels uncomfortable. With bodhicitta, from the moment you begin to open, you feel incredibly peaceful and you get tremendous pleasure and inexhaustible energy. Forget about enlightenment—as soon as you begin to open yourself to others, you gain tremendous pleasure and satisfaction. Working for others is very interesting; it's an infinite activity. Your life becomes continuously rich and interesting.

You can see how easily Western people get bored; as a result, they take drugs and so forth. They are easily bored; they can't see what else to do. It's not that people who take drugs are necessarily unintelligent. They do have intelligence, but they don't know where to put their energy so that it is beneficial to society and themselves. They're blocked; they can't see. Therefore, they destroy themselves.

If you don't want to understand bodhicitta as an attitude dedicated to others—and sometimes it can be difficult to understand it in that way—you can also think of it as a selfish attitude. Why? In practice, when you begin to open yourself to others, you find that your heart is completely tied; your "I," or your ego, is tied. Lama Je Tsong Khapa [in his *Three Principal Aspects of the Path*] described the ego as an "iron net of self-grasping." How do you loosen these bonds? When you begin to dedicate yourself to others, you yourself experience unbelievable peace, unbelievable relaxation. Therefore, I'm saying, with the selfish attitude [of wanting to experience that peace and relaxation], you can practice dedicating yourself to others.

What really matters is your attitude. If your attitude is one of openness and dedication to all universal living beings, it is enough to relax you. In my opinion, having an attitude of bodhicitta is much more powerful—and much more practical in a Western environment—than squeezing yourself in meditation.

Anyway, our twentieth century lives don't allow us time for meditation. Even if we try, we're sluggish. "I was up too late last night; yesterday I worked so hard…." I really believe that the strong, determined, dedicated attitude of "Every day, for the rest of my life, and especially today, I will dedicate myself to others as much as I possibly can," is very powerful. Anyway, some people's attitude towards meditation is that they want some kind of concrete concentration [right now]. It's not possible to develop concrete concentration in a short time without putting your life together. And Westerners find it is very difficult to put their lives together; it's the most difficult thing. Of course, this is just the projection of a Tibetan monk! However, if you don't organize your life, how can you be a good meditator? It's not possible. How can you have good meditation if your life is in disorder?

I don't know what I'm saying! I think I'd better control myself!

EMPTINESS

The next topic is shunyata. But don't worry; His Holiness is going to explain shunyata. However, what I am going to say is that these three—renunciation, bodhicitta and the wisdom of universal reality—are the essence of Buddhism, the essence of Christianity; the essence of universal religion. There's no contradiction at all. Westerners easily rationalize that when a Buddhist monk talks about these three topics, he's on an Eastern trip, but these topics are neither Eastern culture nor Tibetan culture.

Historically, Shakyamuni Buddha taught the four noble truths. To whose culture do the four noble truths belong? The essence of religion has nothing to do with any one particular country's culture. Compassion, love, reality—to whose culture do they belong? The people of any country, any nation, can implement the three principal aspects of the path, the four noble truths or the eightfold path. There's no contradiction at all.

Also, you have to understand that the transmission of these three principal aspects of the path was passed from Lord Manjushri to Lama Tsong Khapa and from Lama Tsong Khapa down to the present time. It's not some exclusive Gelugpa thing; all four Tibetan traditions contain these three principles. Do not hold the misconception that the four traditions practice differently. You can't say that Kagyu, Gelug, Sakya and Nyingma renunciations are different; that Gelug refuge is different from Kagyu refuge. How can you say that? Even if Shakyamuni Buddha comes here and says, "They're different," I'm going to reject what he says. Even if Shakyamuni manifests here, radiating light, saying, "They're different," I'm going to reply, "No, they're not."

People are easily deluded; they hallucinate easily. The first and only thing you have to do in order to become a Buddhist is to take refuge in Buddha, Dharma and Sangha; that's all. How, then, can you say that Gelug refuge and Kagyu refuge are different? I want you to understand this. We have very limited concepts, limited orientation. I want you to see how limited human beings are.

Let me give you an example. Vietnamese Buddhists cannot visualize a Tibetan Buddha. Tibetans cannot visualize a Chinese Buddha. It is very difficult for Westerners to visualize a Japanese Buddha. Does that mean you ignore all these other Buddhas? Does that mean you discriminate, "I take refuge in only Tibetan Buddhas"? Or, "I take refuge in only Western Buddhas. I give up Eastern Buddhas; I give up Japanese Buddhas." Do you understand how we are limited? This is what I call human beings' limitation. They cannot understand things on the universal level and project in a culturally limited way so that their ego has something to hang on to; the Buddha that each nation's Buddhists hang on to is but an object of their ego-grasping.

Also, I've checked Western people out scientifically. Many Westerners have studied Tibetan thangka painting and the Buddhas they create are completely different. The Buddhas they paint are completely westernized, even though the dimensions are fixed precisely according to the Tibetan style and the examples they copy are also Tibetan. This is my scientific experience. This shows that human do things through only their own limited experience.

Anyway, I think it is such a pity that Gelugpas don't want to take refuge in objects that Nyingmapas also take refuge in, such as Padmasambhava. It's written in many Gelug Tibetan texts that

Lama Je Tsong Khapa was a manifestation of Padmasambhava. Maybe I can also say that Lama Je Tsong Khapa was a manifestation of Jesus.

Well, I tell you, misconceptions can arise from when you first take refuge. But you have to learn that taking refuge is not simple; it's very profound. If, at the very beginning, you take refuge with a fanatical understanding of Buddha, Dharma and Sangha, you freak out; you become a Buddhist fanatic. If you are truly Buddhist, my advice is to take refuge in the buddhas and bodhisattvas of the ten directions. In the ten directions there's no division into west or east. Sometimes I think that orientation through the eye sense is not so good. Anyway, Buddha and Dharma are not objects of the eye sense.

The Christian way of explaining God as something universal and omnipresent is good. Actually, that's a good way of understanding things—better than "*My* Buddha; *my* Dharma; *my* Sangha." That's rubbish! That itself is the problem. If you get attached to the particular object of "my lama" or "my things," it's ridiculous. Buddha himself said that we should not be attached to him, or to enlightenment, or to the six paramitas. We should not be attached to anything.

Well, time's almost up. I still feel it's unfortunate that His Holiness could not come. I really feel that inviting His Holiness is like having a second Buddha come to this earth. Therefore, it is unfortunate that he cannot be here and you have to put up with such garbage—an ordinary person like me.

MEDITATION

But let's meditate for a couple of minutes. Send out our white, radiant light energy to purify all obstacles. Especially from our heart, we are sending white, blissful radiating light energy to His Holiness.

[Meditation.]

And from His Holiness the Dalai Lama's heart, a white radiating light OM MANI PADME HUM mantra comes to our heart.

[Meditation.]

Our entire nervous system, from our feet up to our crown, is purified by the OM MANI PADME HUM mantra coming from His Holiness's heart.

[Meditation.]

THE THREE PRINCIPAL ASPECTS
OF THE PATH

SECOND TEACHING: EMPTINESS

Good afternoon. Again, unfortunately, I have to come here and talk nonsense to you. However, I heard that His Holiness is feeling much better this afternoon.

This morning I spoke very generally on the subjects of renunciation and bodhicitta. Now, this time, I will talk about the wisdom of shunyata.

From the Buddhist point of view, having renunciation of samsara and loving kindness bodhicitta alone is not enough to cut the root of the ego or the root of the dualistic mind. By meditating on and practicing loving kindness bodhicitta, you can eliminate gross attachment and feelings of craving, but the root of craving desire and attachment are ego and the dualistic mind. Therefore, without understanding shunyata, or non-duality, it is not possible to cut the root of human problems.

It's like this example: if you have some boiling water and put cold water or ice into it, the boiling water calms down, but you haven't totally extinguished the water's potential to boil.

For example, all of us have a certain degree of loving kindness in our relationships, but many times our loving kindness is a mixture—half white, half black. This is very important. Many times we start with a white, loving kindness motivation but then slowly, slowly it gets mixed up with "black magic" love. Our love starts with pure motivation but as time passes, negative minds arise and our love becomes mixed with black love, dark love. It begins at first as white love but then transforms into black magic love.

I want you to understand that this is due to a lack of wisdom—your not having the penetrative wisdom to go beyond your relative projection. You can see that that's why even religious motivations and religious actions become a mundane trip when you lack penetrative wisdom. That's why Buddhism does not have a good feeling towards fanatical, or emotional, love. Many Westerners project, "Buddhism has no love." Actually, love has nothing to do with emotional expression. The emotional expression of love is so gross; so gross—not refined. Buddhism has tremendous concern for, or understanding of, the needs of both the object and the subject, and in this way, loving kindness becomes an antidote to the selfish attitude.

Western religions also place tremendous emphasis on love and compassion but they do not emphasize wisdom. Understanding wisdom is the path to liberation, so you have to gain it.

Now, as far as emotion is concerned, I think for the Western world, emotion is a big thing, for some reason. However, when we react to or relate with the sense world, we should somehow learn to go the middle way.

When I was in Spain with His Holiness, we visited a monastery and met a Christian monk who had vowed to stay in an isolated place. His Holiness asked him a question, something like,

"How do you feel when you experience signs of happy or unhappy things coming to you?" The monk said something like, "Happy is not necessarily happy; bad is not necessarily bad; good is not necessarily good." I was astonished; I was very happy. "In the world, bad is not too bad; good is not too good." To my small understanding, that was wisdom. We should all learn from that.

Ask yourself whether or not you can do this. Can you experience things the way this monk did or not? For me, this monk's experience was great. I don't care whether he's enlightened or not. All I care is that he had this fantastic experience. It was helpful for his life; I'm sure he was blissful. Anyway, all worldly pleasures and bad experiences are so transitory—knowing their transitory nature, their relative nature, their conventional nature, makes you free.

The person who has some understanding of shunyata will have exactly the same experiences as that priest had. The person sees that bad and good are relative; they exist for only the conditioned mind and are not absolute qualities. The characteristic of ego is to project such fantasy notions onto yourself and others—this is the main root of problems. You then react emotionally and hold as concrete your pleasure and your pain.

You can observe right now how your ego mind interprets yourself, how your self-image is simply a projection of your ego. You can check right now. It's worth checking. The way you check has nothing to do with the sensory mind, your sense consciousness. Close your eyes and check right now. It's a simple question—you don't need to query the past or the future—just ask yourself right now, "How does my mind imagine myself?"

[Meditation.]

You don't need to search for the absolute. It's enough to just ask about your conventional self.

[Meditation.]

Understanding your conventional mind and the way it projects your own self-image is the key to realizing shunyata. In this way you break down the gross concepts of ego and eradicate the self-pitying image of yourself.

[Meditation.]

By eliminating the self-pitying imagination of ego, you go beyond fear. All fear and other self-pitying emotions come from holding a self-pitying image of yourself.

[Meditation.]

You can also see how you feel that yesterday's self-pitying image of yourself still exists today. It's wrong.

[Meditation.]

Thinking, "I'm a very bad person today because I was angry yesterday, I was angry last year," is also wrong, because you are still holding today an angry, self-pitying image from the past. You are not angry today. If that logic were correct, then Shakyamuni Buddha would also be bad, because when he was on earth, he had a hundred wives but was still dissatisfied!

Our ego holds a permanent concept of our ordinary self all the time—this year, last year, the year before: "I'm a bad person; me, me, me, me, me, me." From the Buddhist point of view, that's wrong. If you hold that kind of concept throughout your lifetime—you become a bad person because you *interpret* yourself as a bad person.

Therefore, your ego's interpretation is unreasonable. It has nothing whatsoever to do with reality. And because your ego holds onto such a self-existent I, attachment begins.

I remember His Holiness once giving an audience to about twenty or thirty monks at a Christian monastery and His Holiness asking one of the monks, "What is your interpretation of emptiness?" One of them answered, "From the Christian point of view, non-attachment is shunyata." What do you think about that? For me, somebody's having an experience of non-attachment is super. Don't you think it's super? Attachment is a symptom of this sick world. This world is sick because of attachment. Do you understand? The Middle East is sick because of attachment. Oil-producing countries are sick because of attachment. Am I communicating with you or not? And that Christian monk experienced non-attachment. What do you think of that?

From the Buddhist point of view, it is very difficult for a person to experience non-attachment; it's very difficult. For that reason, for me, it is extremely good if somebody—even somebody from another religion—experiences it. And that, too, is a reason for having the confidence to respect other religions.

How many Buddhists here have experienced non-attachment? None? Surprise, surprise! Well, excuse me; I'm just joking. But it is very important to have the experience of non-attachment; it is very important for all of us.

Now, I want you to understand what attachment means. We can use this piece of electrician's tape as an example. From the Buddhist philosophical point of view, attachment for something means that it's very difficult for us to separate from it. In this example, the attachment of the electrician's tape is no problem because it is easy to loosen, easy to reattach and easy to loosen again. But, we have a very strong attachment—strong like iron—for the things we think of as being very good. So, we need to learn to be flexible.

Let's look at this flower from the Buddhist point of view. My attachment for the flower is a symptom. It shows that I overestimate the value of the flower. I wish to become one with the flower and never separate from it for the rest of my life. You understand now, how sick I am? It is so difficult for me to let go of it. What do you think? Am I crazy? This craziness is attachment. But, non-attachment is flexible; it is a middle way, a reasonable way. Let go.

Do you understand? The psychology of attachment is over-estimation; it is an unrealistic attitude. That's why we are suffering;

and for that reason Buddhism emphasizes suffering, suffering, suffering.

The Western point of view is that Buddhism overemphasizes suffering. Westerners can't understand why Buddhism talks about suffering so much. "I have enough money. I can eat. I have enough clothes. Why do you say I'm suffering? I'm not suffering. I don't need Buddhism." Many Westerners say this kind of thing. This is a misunderstanding of the term "suffering." The nature of attachment is suffering.

Look at Western society. The biggest problem in the West is attachment. It's so simple. From birth, through school and up to professorship, or whatever one achieves, the Western life is built by attachment. Of course, it's not only the Western life— attachment characterizes the life of each and every sentient being—but why I'm singling out the West is because Westerners sometimes have funny ideas about the connotation of happiness and suffering.

Philosophically, of course, you can research shunyata very deeply; you can analyze the notion of the self-existent I a thousand ways. But here I'm talking about what you can do practically, every day, right now, in a simple way. Don't think about Buddhist terminology; don't think about what the books say or anything like that. Just ask yourself simply, "How, at this moment, do I interpret myself?" That's all.

Each time you ask yourself that question you get a different answer, I tell you. Because sometimes you're emanating as a chicken; sometimes as a pig; sometimes as a monkey. Then you can laugh at yourself: "What I'm thinking is incredible! I'm a pig." But you shouldn't worry when you see yourself as a pig. Don't worry; just laugh. The way you check, the way you question yourself, should just make you laugh. In that way you get closer to shunyata. Because you know something—through your own experience, you know that your own projection of yourself is a fantasy and, to some extent, you experience selflessness. You no longer trust your own ego, and your concepts become less concrete.

Analytical meditation shouldn't make you sad or serious. When you really understand something, you can laugh at yourself. Of course, if you're alone, you shouldn't laugh out loud too much, otherwise people will think you're clinically sick! Milarepa is a good example. He stayed alone in the snowy mountains and laughed and sang to himself. What do you think about that? Do you think he was sick? No. He laughed because his life was rich and he was happy.

Your entire life is built by dualistic concepts. If it's not, you can't function in society, in the relative world. In order to become a part of normal society, you have to develop incredible dualistic concepts. Many of the things in this world that we consider to be knowledge, wisdom and education are aspects of the dualistic mind; the reaction they bring is just more suffering.

What is the dualistic mind? Actually, "dual" means two, but in Buddhism, our complaint is not that two phenomena exist. The problem is their contradictory, competitive nature. Is the competitive mind comfortable or not? Is the competitive life comfortable or not? Is competitive business comfortable or not?

The mind is irritated. The mind in which there are two things always contradicting each other is what we call the dualistic mind.

Simply put, when you get up in the morning after a good night's sleep, do you feel peaceful or not? Yes, you feel peaceful. Why? Because during sleep, the dualistic mind is at rest—to some extent!

As long as the dualistic mind is functioning in your life, you are always irritated; you have not attained the peace of ultimate reality. That's why single-pointed concentration is very useful. Single-pointed concentration is very useful for cutting the gross dualistic mind, especially when you want to recognize and contemplate on your own consciousness. It's very powerful for eliminating dualistic concepts. This is what is taught in Tibetan *mahamudra,* or *dzog-chen.*

The purpose of meditation is to stop the irritating concepts that we call dualistic mind. Of course, there are many levels to this. The dualistic mind has many gross levels and many subtle levels, and the way to eliminate it is to start with the gross [and progress to the subtle].

But now I don't know what I'm talking about, so instead of my going on, "Blah, blah, blah," why don't we do some questions and answers? If I keep on talking, I'm sure I'll just create more confusion—more dualistic mind—for you. Therefore, it's better that we have a question and answer session.

Q: If you think that detachment is necessary, non-attachment is necessary, why should we be attached to one philosophy?
Lama: We should not be attached to any philosophy. We should

not be attached to any religion. We should not have any objects of attachment. We should not be attached to God. We should not be attached to the Bible. We should not be attached to Buddha. That's very good. Thank you; that's a very good question. That question is very important. It shows us the character of Buddhism. Buddhism has no room for you to be attached to something, for you to grasp at something. Buddha said even grasping at or having attachment to Buddha is wrong. As long as you are sick, even if you possess diamonds, you are still sick. All symptoms of attachment have to vanish for you to become a completely liberated human being. For that reason, Buddhism has room for any philosophy, any religion, any trip—as long as it is beneficial for human growth.

Q: What is the difference between attachment and compassion?
Lama: Compassion understands others' lack of pleasure and their suffering situation. Attachment is "I want; I want"—concern for our own pleasure. Compassion is concern for others' pleasure and the determination to release other sentient beings from their problems. But many times we mix our compassion with attachment. We begin with compassion but after some time attachment mixes in and it then becomes an attachment trip. Thank you; thank you so much.

Q: Are non-duality and bodhicitta the same thing?
Lama: No. Remember what I said at the beginning: it is not enough to have just renunciation and loving kindness bodhicitta. That's not enough for us. We need wisdom to cut through

dualistic concepts and see the universal reality behind them. This is very important. Without wisdom, our bodhicitta and love can become fanatical. If we understand non-duality, it's all right—bodhicitta can develop easily.

[*The following three paragraphs are not on the video:*]

Q: There's a Zen koan that says if you see the Buddha on the road, kill him. Would the interpretation of this be that if you see the Buddha on the road, you have attachment to Buddha, so kill the attachment, not the Buddha?

Lama: No. But this can be interpreted in many different ways. Let's say I see you as the Buddha. I probably have an incredible projection, so it's better that I kill that. First of all, the way to seek the Buddha is not outside. The Buddha is within; that's where we should seek. When we begin, we seek in the wrong place. That's what we should kill. But we should not kill like Jim Jones did, by poisoning his followers.

Q: Is it enough if we stop the conceptualization of the mind so that the "I" ceases to exist?

Lama: Yes. For practical purposes, yes. But philosophically, it's not so clear. Practically speaking, whether we talk a lot about it or not, we know that in our own lives, it is extremely difficult to stop our obsessed concepts. And we are not flexible. Therefore, it is better to stop them as much as you can, but you can't stop them completely, just like that—unless you completely extinguish yourself.

Q: Is mantra important to destroy the ego?

Lama: Yes. But of course, it has to be an individual experience. By the time you're a first stage bodhisattva, you no longer need mantra. Then, there's no such thing as an external mantra. You yourself become the nuclear essence of mantra, because at that time you have discovered the absolute mantra. At the moment, we play around with the relative mantra, but let's hope that we eventually discover the absolute mantra.

Q: I understood from what you said before that emotions are negative, but is not the quality of the emotions the qualities of the person, him- or herself?

Lama: I said if your daily life is tremendously involved in emotion, you are completely driven by them and psychologically tied. Therefore, you have to learn to sit back instead of being impelled by your emotions. Also, I did not say that emotions are necessarily negative. Emotions can be positive too. But what I'm saying—and I'm making a generalization—is that in the Western environment, when we relate with each other we get tremendously emotional. In other words, our physical emotions get too involved and we don't understand the functioning of our six sense consciousnesses.

Q: How can we live without attachment and without desire? It's too difficult.

Lama: I agree with you! Yes. It's too difficult. That's why we human beings do not find it easy to develop responsible attitudes and stop our own problems—we need to be involved in doing this our entire life. Being mindful, being conscious, is not an easy job. You're right. But there's a way to transform desire, a way to transform attachment. In that way, the energy of desire and attachment becomes medicine, the path to liberation. It's like when you mix poison with certain other medicines it can become medicine. What is an example? Marijuana and hashish can be medicine, can't they? They may not be good, but when you can transform their energy they can become medicine. That is the beauty of the human being; we have powerful methods for transforming one thing into something else.

Tibetan Buddhism has many methods for transforming desire and attachment into the path to liberation. We place great emphasis on these methods. Red chili, for example, is not so good alone, but when you mix reasonable quantities of it with your food, it becomes delicious.

Therefore, I want you to understand this question. According to the Buddhist point of view, there is no human problem that cannot be solved by human beings. Each one of you should understand this personally and encourage yourself by thinking, "I can deal with all my problems; I can solve my problems." That attitude is essential for your spiritual growth. Even though we may not be much good as meditators or spiritual practitioners, I truly believe that if we have some understanding and encouragement, we can all solve our problems. Most of the time, we fail to understand our own capacity. We put ourselves down. That's why in Tibetan Buddhism we see ourselves as Buddha. I'm sure you've all heard that kind of thing. [*Video ends here.*] Don't make a tremendous gap by thinking that Buddha is way up in the sky and you are way underneath the earth. That is good enough.

Thank you; I won't take up any more of your time. Thank you so much.

INTRODUCTION TO TANTRA

INTRODUCTION TO TANTRA

FIRST TEACHING

Maybe we are going to practice tantric yoga, but it's not easy to do. In order to practice tantric yoga we need a foundation—the preliminaries. First of all, in order to practice tantric yoga, we need to receive an empowerment, or initiation. There are degrees of initiation, but we do need initiation. In order to receive an initiation, we need a certain extent of realization of the three principal paths to enlightenment, which are the wisdom of shunyata, bodhicitta and renunciation. Therefore, it is not easy.

When I say it's not easy, the sense is not that it's a difficult job in terms of money. I mean it's difficult because of our present level. I'm saying it's difficult to practice tantric yoga without a proper foundation, without the right qualifications. Why is it difficult? Because of our level. If we check out our own reality, our present situation, do we have some kind of small understanding of the reality of our own mind? The nature of the mind has two aspects—its relative nature and its absolute nature. Do we know our own mind's relative nature? If we know the relative nature of our own mind, it's easy to direct our mind's attitude. That is each individual's responsibility to check out.

Then, there's bodhicitta. Bodhicitta is a heart that's open to other people rather than totally closed. I'm not talking from the philosophical point of view: "You should be open to other people; if you are closed, I'm going to beat you." I'm not talking that way. If you are not open, the symptoms are great—you suffer a great deal, you're in conflict with yourself and you experience much confusion and dissatisfaction—as you already know; as you already experience every day.

The sense of being open is also not so that others will give you presents, that you'll get chocolate cake. That's not the way, although normally we are like that. Of course, we are not buddha, but to some extent we should have an inner, deep, perhaps intellectual understanding, some discriminating wisdom, that the human need is not simply temporal pleasure. To some extent, we all have temporal pleasure, but what we really need is eternal peace. Having that highest of destinations is the way to be open. It eliminates the problems of everyday life—we don't get upset if someone doesn't give us some small thing. Normally we do. Our problem is expectation. We grasp at such small, unworthy things. That grasping mind is the problem; it produces the symptom of reacting again and again and again. Last year we reacted in a negative way and this year, it's the same or worse. That's how it seems. We're supposed to get better and better but our problems are still overwhelming.

Philosophically, perhaps we can say that karma is overwhelming—consciously and unconsciously. Don't think that karma is just your doing something consciously and then ending up miserable. Karma also functions at the unconscious level. You can do something unconsciously and it can still lead to a big result. Today's problems in the Middle East are a good example. That's karma. They started off small, but those little actions have brought a huge result. As a matter of fact, that's karma.

In order to have the enlightened attitude, an attitude that transcends the self-pitying thought, you need the tremendous energy of renunciation of temporary pleasure—renunciation of samsara. I think you know this already. What do we renounce? Samsara. Therefore, we call it renunciation of samsara. Now I'm sure you're getting scared! Renunciation of samsara is the right attitude. The wrong attitude is that which is opposite to renunciation.

You probably think, "Oh, that's too difficult." It's not difficult. You do have renunciation. How many times do you reject certain situations, unpleasant situations? That's you renouncing. Birds and dogs have renunciation. Children have renunciation—if they want to do something for which they'll get punished, they know how to get around it. That's their way of renunciation. But all that is not renunciation of samsara. Perhaps your heart is broken because of some trouble with a friend so you change your relationship. Anyway, your friend has already given you up so you have to do the same thing and renounce your friend. Neither is that renunciation of samsara.

Perhaps you're having trouble coping with society so you escape into the bush, like an animal. You're renouncing something, but that's not renunciation of samsara.

What, then, is renunciation of samsara? Be careful now—it's not being obsessed with the objects of samsaric existence or with nirvana, either. Perhaps some people will think, "Now that I'm not concerned with pleasure, now that I'm renounced, I would like to have pain." That, too, is not renunciation of samsara. Renouncing the sense pleasures of the desire realm and looking for something else instead, grasping at the pleasures of the form or formless realms, is still the same old samsaric trip.

Say you're practicing meditation, Buddhist philosophy and so forth and somebody tells you, "What you're doing is garbage; nobody in this country understands those things." If somebody puts the nail of criticism into you like that and you react by getting agitated and angry, it means that your trip of Buddhism, meditation or whatever is also samsaric. It has nothing to do with renunciation of samsara. That's a problem, isn't it? You're practicing meditation, Buddhism; you think Buddha is special, but when somebody says, "Buddha is not special," you get shocked. That means you're not free; you're clinging. You have not put your mind into the right atmosphere. There's still something wrong in your mind.

So, renunciation of samsara is not easy. For you, at the moment, it's only words, but the thing is that renunciation of samsara is the mind that deeply renounces, or is deeply detached from, all existent phenomena. You think what I'm talking about is only an idea, but in order for the human mind to be healthy, you should not have the neurotic symptom of grasping at any object whatsoever, be it pleasure or suffering. Then, relaxation will be there; that is relaxation. You don't have superstition pumping you up. We should all have healthy minds by eliminating all objects that obsess the ego. All objects. We are so concrete that even when we come to Buddhism or meditation, they also become concrete. We have to break our concrete preconceptions, and that can only be done by the clean clear mind.

For example, when you see an old tree in the distance and think that it's a human being, your superstitious mind is holding that wood as a human being. In order to eliminate your ego's wrong conception, you have to see that collection of energy as wood. If you see that clean clear, the conception holding that object as a human being will disappear. It's the same thing: the clean clear mind is the solution that eliminates all concrete wrong conceptions.

Because our conceptions are concrete, we are not flexible. Somebody says, "Let's do it this way," but you don't want to change. Only you are right; other people are wrong.

Tied by this kind of grasping at samsaric phenomena at the conception level, it is difficult for you to see the possibility of achieving a higher destination. You are trapped in your present limited situation and can see no way out of it.

Practically, renunciation means being easygoing—not too much sense pleasure and not so much freaking out. Even if you have some pain, there's an acceptance of it. The pain is already there; you can't reject it. The pain is already there, but you're easygoing about it.

Perhaps it's better if I put it this way—you're easygoing with the eight worldly dharmas. I think you already know what they are. If you are easygoing with them, that's good enough. You should not think that renunciation is important simply from the Buddhist philosophical point of view in order to reach liberation. Renunciation is not just an idea; you should understand renunciation correctly.

Shakyamuni himself appeared on this earth. He had a kingdom; he had a mother and a father; he drank milk. Still, he was renounced. There was no problem. For him, drinking milk was not a problem—ideologically, philosophically. But *we* have a problem.

Another way of saying all this is that practicing Buddhism is not like soup. We should approach Buddhadharma organically, gradually; we are fulfilled gradually. You can't practice Dharma like going to a supermarket, where in one visit you can take everything you want simultaneously. Dharma practice is something personal, unique. You do just what you need to do to put your mind into the right atmosphere. That is important.

Perhaps I can say something like this: Americans practice Dharma without comprehension of the karmic actions of body, speech and mind. American renunciation is to grasp at the highest pleasures; Americans try to become bodhisattvas without renunciation of samsara! Is that possible? Perhaps you can't take any more of this! Still, be careful. I'm saying that there's no bodhisattva without realization of renunciation. Please, excuse my aggression! Well, the world is full of aggression, so some of it has rubbed off on me.

Of course, actually, we are very fortunate. Just trying to practice Dharma is very fortunate. But also, it's good to know how the gradual path to enlightenment is set up in a very personal way.

It's not just structured according to the object. If you know this, it becomes very tasty. Of course we can't become bodhisattvas all of a sudden, but if you can get a clean clear overview of the path's gradual progression, you'll approach it without confusion.

Dharma brothers and sisters are often confused because of the Dharma supermarket. There are so many things to choose from. After a while you don't know what's good for you. The first time I went to an American supermarket I was confused; I didn't know what I should buy and what I shouldn't. So, it's similar. You should have clean clear understanding. Then you can act in the right direction with confidence.

So, you should not regard the three principal paths to enlightenment as a philosophical phenomenon. You should feel that they are there according to your own organic need.

If you hunger for sentimental temporal pleasure, it's not so good. You don't have a big mind. Your mind is very narrow. You should know that pleasure is transitory, impermanent, coming and going, coming and going like a Californian friend—going, coming, going! When you have renunciation, you somehow lose your fanatical, over-sensitive expectations. Then you experience less suffering, your attitude is less neurotic, and you have fewer expectations and less frustration.

Basically, frustration is built up by superstition, the samsaric attitude, which is the opposite of renunciation of samsara. Following that, you always end up unbalanced and trapped in misery. We know this. So, you should see it clean clear. That is the purpose of meditation. Meditation is not on the level of the object but on that of the subject—*you* are the business of your meditation.

The beauty of meditation is that you can understand your own reality, and if you understand your own problems in this way, you can understand all living beings' situation. But if you don't understand your own reality, there's no way you can understand others, no matter how hard you try—"I want to understand what's going on with my friend"—you can't. You don't even understand what's going on in your own mind. So, meditation is experimenting to see what's happening in your own mind, to know the nature of your own mind. Then, as Nagarjuna said, if you understand your own mind, you understand the whole thing. You don't need to put effort into trying to understand what's going on with each person individually. You don't need to do that.

We talk about human problems; we talk about our own problems every day of our lives. The reason I have a problem with you is because I want something from you. If I didn't want something from you, I wouldn't have a problem with you. That's why the lam-rim teaches that attachment, grasping at your own pleasure, is the source of pain and misery, and being open, concerned for other people's pleasure, is the source of happiness, realization and success. For some reason, it's true; even on the materialistic level. I tell you, actually—forget for a moment about Buddhadharma and the universal sentient beings—even if you simply want good business, somehow, if you have a broad view and want to help other people—your family, your nation— somehow, for some reason, you will be successful. On the other hand, if you are only concerned for "me, me, me, me, me," always crying that "me" is the most important thing, you'll fail, even materially. It's true; even material success will not be possible.

Many people, even in this country, have material problems because they are concerned for only themselves. Even though society offers many good situations, they are still in the preta realm. I think so, isn't it? You are living in America but you're still living in the preta realm—of the three lower realms, the hungry ghost realm; you are still living in the hungry ghost realm.

Psychologically, this is very important. Don't think that I'm just talking about something philosophical: "You should help other people; you should help other people." I'm saying that if you want to be happy, eradicate your attachment; cut your concrete concepts. The way to cut them is not troublesome—just change your attitude; switch your attitude, that's all. It's not really a big deal! It's really skillful, reasonable. The way Buddhism explains this is reasonable. It's not something in which you have to super-believe. I'm not saying you have to try to be a superwoman or superman. It's reasonable and logical. Simply changing your attitude eliminates your concrete concepts.

Remember equilibrium? Equilibrium does not mean that I equalize you externally. If that were so, then you'd have to come to Nepal and eat only rice and dhal. Equilibrium is not to do with the object, it's to do with the subject; it's *my* business. My two extreme minds—desire, the overestimated view and grabbing, and hatred, the underestimated view and rejecting—conflict, destroying my own peace, happiness and loving kindness. In order to balance those two, I have to actualize equilibrium.

The minute your fanatical view and grasping start, the reaction of hatred has already arrived. They come together. I think you have experienced this; we do have experience. The minute something becomes special for you, breaks your heart, in that minute, the opposite mind of hatred has come. They are inter-dependent phenomena. For some reason, by having an ego, the tendency is always to be unbalanced, extreme. We have so many problems—individual, personal problems; they all come from the extreme mind.

Actually, you should pray not to have desirable objects of the fanatical view. You're better off without them. They are the symptoms of a broken heart and lead to restlessness. You should be reasonable.

You can see that some people's relationships are reasonable. Therefore, they last for a long time. If people's relationships start off extreme, how can they last? You know from the beginning, they cannot last. Balance is so important.

The thing is, *why* don't we have good meditation? Simply—why don't we have good meditation? Why can't we concentrate, even for a minute? Because our extreme mind explodes; internally, there's a nuclear blow-up. That's all. We're out of control. We should learn how to handle that explosion.

First of all, this problem is not something that has happened by accident. We should know that there's an evolution to its existence. Therefore, our first order of business should be to investigate the extreme view of our ego mind.

Now, I'm going to go quickly. This morning you did the meditation of contemplating on your breath in an easygoing way. But as meditators, we are also extreme. The reason is that samsara is so overwhelming and our reaction is, "I *want* to meditate; I *should* meditate." We push and push, pump and pump; we're very unnatural. That's no good. Then our minds freak out. Then we don't like coming to the meditation center; we want to escape to the jungle. We make ourselves like that; we beat our mind. That is unskillful. It's true. I think most meditators are unskillful—like me. Unskillful.

The thing is, saying it another way, we are *too intellectual*. Even though we don't learn intellectual philosophy, we are still intellectual. Intellectually, we push ourselves this way and that. It's unnatural. We are unnatural. That's the problem. We are so artificial. We're artificial, plastic intellectuals; we're a new type of plastic product—plastic intellectuals!

We should be happy. Approaching Dharma, approaching meditation, we can be happy. It means we want to be happy. We know we all want to be happy, but we often misunderstand lam-rim and Dharma. We think that when we come to Buddhism, we should suffer; our lives should be ascetic; we should be mean to ourselves. That should not be the case. You love yourself, you have compassion for yourself, so you should not put in tremendous, tight effort when you meditate. You should *not* put in tremendous effort! You should learn to let go. Actually, it's true—meditation is easygoing; using simple language, it's easygoing.

So, contemplate your breath without expecting good things to happen or bad things to happen. Anyway, at that time, it's too late to be concerned whether good or bad things are going to happen. Whatever comes comes; whatever doesn't come doesn't come. At that moment, you can't do anything about it. So, contemplate your breath. Now, when you reach the point where maybe there are neither good thoughts nor bad thoughts, just medium, it means you're successful. At that time, according to your level, just let go; let go. Have no expectations of what's happening, what's going to happen, what's really happening—no expectations. Just let go.

When distractions come—perhaps your ego imagines, "Oh, I'm getting pleasure"—don't reject them; contemplate such notions. In that way, you can reach the point where the first notion disappears, which shows that the appearances your ego imagines are false. When they clear, contemplate the resultant clarity. If you are unable to contemplate that clarity, move your mind a little by thinking, "I have just caught my ego muddying my mind with illusions and overestimated conceptions; so many living beings suffer from such conceptions and are unable to catch them as I can," and generate much compassion or bodhicitta. You can also generate the determination to release other sentient beings from that ignorance, while being aware that, "At the moment, I don't have the ability to really lead other sentient beings into clarity, therefore, I need to clear up my own mind more."

Then go back to contemplating your own thought again. Through your own experience, you know that your mind, or thought, or consciousness, has no color or form. Its nature is like a clean clear mirror that reflects any phenomenon. That is your mind, your consciousness, your thought. The essence of thought is perfect clarity. The movement of thought creates conflict, but when you investigate the nature of the subject, you find that the essential character of thought, even bad thought, is still perfect clarity. It is clean clear, like a mirror, and reflects even irritating objects. Therefore, when even bad thoughts come, don't get upset, don't cry, and don't criticize yourself—instead, use the technique of simply being aware; just contemplate the clarity of the subject, your own mind. If you do that, it will again become clear, because clarity is its nature. Similarly, when good thoughts come, instead of getting busily distracted by the object, again contemplate the clarity of the subject, your own mind.

Another way of saying this is that when you have a problem of thinking, "This is a good thought; this is a bad thought," remember that in fact, both types of thought are unified in having clarity as their nature. If I pour two glasses of water into one container and shake it up, the water looks disturbed but the nature of the water from both glasses is still clean clear. Shaking them up together doesn't turn the water into fire; it still retains its clean clear water energy.

Sometimes it looks complicated when we present the three principal paths to enlightenment in the Tibetan way, but actually, they're very simple. When you are contemplating and a thought arises, move from that thought and practice renunciation. When another thought comes, move from that to bodhicitta. Then again go back and contemplate the clarity of your own consciousness. That's easy—you're just moving your mind into renunciation, bodhicitta or shunyata. You're doing well! You're making your life worthwhile.

When we explain the lam-rim, we can go into so much detail. You can explain renunciation so extensively that you could spend thirty days talking about renunciation alone; and thirty days on bodhicitta alone; and thirty days on shunyata alone. Maybe we need all that, but when you're practicing, you can put those three together such that just one movement of your mind becomes renunciation; one movement becomes bodhicitta; one movement becomes shunyata. You can do this. Sometimes when we give extensive explanations you think, "Wow; this is too much." But if you put it practically, when you practice, the lam-rim can become in some ways small.

Perhaps that's enough for today. However, when you reach the point of clean clear comprehension, just leave your mind on that. Let go and don't intellectualize.

Introduction to Tantra

Second Teaching

When we are seeking liberation, or inner freedom, there are two vehicles, which we call the Hinayana vehicle and the Mahayana vehicle. When somebody is seeking liberation, there are two things. Hinayana and Mahayana are Sanskrit terms, but if we translate their meaning into English, they mean the small attitude and the great attitude.

The small attitude is, well, we already have a small attitude! Especially when we're in trouble: "I want happiness, liberation, freedom." The "I want" attitude leads to small action, small vehicle, small boat. Mahayana means the great attitude; that's what we are trying to do.

When I mention these two vehicles of Hinayana and Mahayana, perhaps you think I'm putting the Hinayana doctrine down. That's not the case. I'm not interested in giving you philosophical comprehension. You already have more philosophical comprehension than a supermarket has stuff. Also, when I talk about Hinayana and Mahayana—small mind and great mind—I'm not talking about doctrine. I'm talking about *us*.

We mean well; we want to practice Mahayana. We'd like to be as open as possible. We want to go that way, even with hardship.

But the narrow mind is overwhelming. It keeps on coming all the time. Maybe intellectually we try to be as open as possible but the narrow mind overwhelms us yet again. Therefore, it is not easy to be a Mahayanist. Both Atisha and Lama Tsong Khapa said that it is not enough for a person's religion to be Mahayana; the person himself or herself must become Mahayana.

This is similar to what a Kadampa geshe once said: "It is not enough that your doctrine is *dzog-chen*; you *yourself* must be *dzog-chen*." *Dzog-chen* means great completion, so he was saying that it is not enough for your doctrine to be complete; you *yourself* must be complete. That's clear, isn't it? Of course, we talk about Mahayana philosophy, so perhaps we can say we are all Mahayana philosophers, because we talk, talk, talk about it. But we are *not* Mahayanists. It is a sort of realization; a level, or state, of mind. Intellectually you can't say, "Oh, today I learned some Mahayana philosophy so I'm a Mahayanist." You can't say that; it's not possible. Until I have solved certain problems, until I have transformed something, until some change has happened in my mind—I'm happier, more open, more satisfied in myself—only then can I say, "I'm a Mahayanist."

Anyway, I don't want to talk too much that way. I'd better attend to the business at hand. In America we don't have time to do so many things, do we? Better make sure we finish.

So, the business at hand is that both Hinayana and Mahayana practitioners are seeking liberation by understanding the nature of samsara, but one of them is making tremendous effort on the basis of, "*I* am the suffering one; *I* cannot stay there in this way. I want to liberate *myself*." The emphasis is on liberating *me*. Great vehicle practitioners, Mahayanists, don't cry so much. Even though they have problems, they are more concerned about other people's problems than their own. That's the difference.

That's why we say that bodhicitta is the door to enter the Mahayana vehicle. That's why bodhicitta is the principal, most essential need for stopping the problem of the self-pitying, self-cherishing thought. Therefore, if you are a Mahayanist, you have bodhicitta. What makes you a bodhisattva is having the realization of bodhicitta.

Then perhaps you will think, "I'm seeking enlightenment; that's why I'm meditating. I *desire* to reach enlightenment; that's why I've come to this meditation course. So how can that be?"

Let me give you an example. Say you are hungry and you go to a restaurant. In some restaurants they have a system where before you can get your food, you have to buy a ticket. Once you have a ticket, then you can get the food. Some places are like that. Your principal aim is to get food to stop your hunger, isn't it? To do that, you have to start by going through the business of getting a ticket. It's the same thing: we are Mahayanists; our job, our duty, is to serve other people. That is our principal aim, not getting enlightenment. We should not cry and grasp, "Enlightenment, enlightenment, enlightenment; I'm unhappy. I want to be happy." That is not principal. Now you can see the difference.

There are two things. A bodhisattva has two goals, two destinations: to help other people and to become self-sufficient by receiving enlightenment, by becoming totality. If we grab that—

"It is more important that I become enlightened"—it's partial. But still we have to do it. It's not the principal thing, it's partial, but we still have to get the ticket in order to solve problems and help other sentient beings. I think this example is clear, isn't it?

Still, some people debate philosophically. The Western mind is sneaky, always intellectualizing this and that. They say that since desire and grasping at sense pleasure is the irritant that leads to the cycle of confusion, one should not wish to get enlightened or to help other people—that that is also desire. Some people argue that way. They say that you're in bondage whether you're bound by wire or by silver or gold; whatever it is that binds you, you're still bound. Therefore, we should be completely free of any kind of wish. Many people say this. Have you heard that kind of thing? That kind of wrong philosophical debate is a waste of time.

They are different. Can you see the difference? Don't be confused about important things. Wishing to open other people, especially to the highest destination, enlightenment, is very important. I think you know this already and I don't need to talk too much about it. So, bodhicitta is the open, enlightened attitude—or, saying it another way, the healthy mind. Instead of using the Sanskrit—the healthy mind. No irritation; plenty of room. That's all. That *is* bodhicitta. *Citta* is Sanskrit; it means mind, in the sense of heart. Heart feeling is what we need. We *need* that attitude, not just an intellectual explanation.

Normally, Western people say, "I need so much love; nobody loves me." They say that kind of thing, don't they? Use that expression in the reverse way: We *need* the totally opened attitude.

It takes care of all the problems that the narrow attitude brings. If you have this attitude you make yourself a complete human being—that's a better way of putting it—because you have complete comprehension. Otherwise, you're in the dark shadow of ignorance. You can see one thing but the rest is in the dark. You *know* that. Even in everyday life, you need some kind of complete comprehension to keep your house and family together. If the husband sees only one thing, he cannot see the totality of his family's needs—especially in America! It's the same thing with the wife. Of course, a woman comprehends things differently than a man does, but again, she sees only one thing and cannot see totality, what is needed for a totally satisfied life or total mental integration.

These examples are very good. Our lifestyle deteriorates because we don't put our life together. We don't see the totality of our needs. When we don't see totality we can't see how everything is interrelated—when we move one thing, everything else moves too. We have to know that.

Anyway, the enlightened attitude of bodhicitta allows your energy to expand universally. You develop a broad view. Now, one who has bodhicitta can follow one of two vehicles, the Paramitayana and the Tantrayana. The Paramitayana is like the lam-rim, where you understand karmic causation and recognize your own profound ability, or potential, to solve completely all levels of ego problem, not just those on the human level. The Paramitayana takes you through the three principal paths to enlightenment and your job is to actualize the six paramitas. You know this already;

I'm just repeating it. That is the Paramitayana. Practicing in that way leads you to enlightenment. But don't think that the enlightenment the Paramitayana path leads you to is a small enlightenment, whereas Tantrayana leads you to a great enlightenment. The enlightened experience that results from following both these yanas is the same; the way they function is where they differ.

Paramitayana and Tantrayana differ in that Tantrayana has the skillful wisdom by which you put totality together. Tantrayana has that kind of key. The Paramitayana also has a key, but its path is slow. The Paramitayana practitioner cannot put two things together simultaneously and keep going. To do that is difficult. Like my cook, Babaji—he can't be in the kitchen and here listening to teachings at the same time! That's his problem. The practitioner of Tantrayana has the skill and intelligence to both see reality clean clear in a penetrative way and simultaneously keep going in a unified way. There's a great difference between the two.

For example, Lord Shakyamuni, the present Buddha, discovered enlightenment after struggling for three countless great eons; three countless great kalpas. Shakyamuni himself made a long journey and led a very ascetic life. Some people say he did not eat for six years; others say he ate the fruit of the palm tree. Palm trees bear fruit [dates]. If we Americans tried to survive on that, we couldn't; we'd die. Back then, maybe the taste was different from what it is today; maybe better than chocolate. Who knows how it was at the time?

There are different explanations about the way he became enlightened. We can't go into detail here; it takes too much time.

However, one explanation is that when he came to earth he was a tenth stage bodhisattva, ready to become enlightened in just a second. And while he was in samadhi during the ascetic phase of his life, other buddhas awoke him from his samadhi, saying, "Hey, what are you doing? You're having a good meditation, but that's not enough for you to expand into totality." So they gave him the four great initiations, including the third and the fourth initiations, and he became enlightened.

So, why did he show that aspect? Normally we say "show" because he was already enlightened before he came to earth and everything he did in his life was just a show.

The reason is that, from the tantric point of view, without practicing tantra, it is not possible to discover enlightenment. Following the Paramitayana alone can take you to only the tenth bodhisattva *bhumi*, or level, and without receiving initiation and practicing tantra, there's no way to achieve enlightenment. This is tantric propaganda! I'm joking! There are many reasons for this, but without practicing tantra, you can't fully open; the extremely subtle mind cannot function. It's something like that.

The difference between Paramitayana and Tantrayana is that the Tantrayana has the skillful methods whereby you can use desire objects that usually bring reactions of confusion and dissatisfaction in the path to enlightenment; by practicing tantric yoga, you can transform the energy of desire into the path to enlightenment. We call it taking desire as the path to enlightenment, but it is dangerous if you do not understand what these words mean; it takes some research to understand them correctly.

Once, during Lord Buddha's time, a king asked him, "As a king, I have so much business to attend to, so many responsibilities in taking care of my nation and so many pleasures. Given my situation, please give me a method to quickly discover enlightenment." Then Shakyamuni gave him the method of Tantrayana.

You can see why Lord Buddha gave the king such teachings from the way he asked, but the person practicing Tantrayana has to have the skill to transform daily pleasures into the path to enlightenment. Let's take our body as an example. As a matter of fact, our body comes from the functioning of desire, doesn't it? Desire made this body; ego made this body. Our grabbing ego made this body manifest, come out. However, instead of looking at it negatively, we should regard it as precious. We know that our body is complicated, but from the Dharma point of view, instead of putting ourselves down with self-pity—"My body is a heavy burden; I wish it would disappear"—we should appreciate and take advantage of it. We should use it in a good way.

So, my example is—I'm not going to miss my example—the point is that despite where the body comes from, the way it manifests, despite the fact that it's not so easygoing, that it's complicated, this body has great ability; it can do so much. With this body, not only can we take care of our food and clothing, but we can also reach beyond that; we have the opportunity to gain the eternal goals of liberation or enlightenment. That's why our human body is precious; that's the point. We can use it in a good way, even though it is potentially poisonous in that it can create more complications, confusion, suffering, loneliness, dissatisfaction and samsaric rebirths for us. If we can change in a positive way, we can feel grateful for having this body and make it worthwhile.

It's similar with our daily pleasures, our sense pleasures. Normally, grasping at sense pleasures brings the reaction of confusion and so forth. We know that. Now, Paramitayana and Tantrayana both lead to enlightenment, but even though at the beginning it might look like contact with sense pleasures is negative, Tantrayana gives us the powerful skill to transmute desire into the blissful path to enlightenment. That's why the wisdom of tantra is perfect.

And especially, when you practice tantra, instead of thinking, "I'm a problem; my ego's a problem; I'm a weak person; I need…" instead of thinking of yourself with self-pity, think, "I am the Buddha; I am Chenrezig; I am universal compassion." The difference is unbelievable. There's a huge difference.

Paramitayana does not have the skillful means whereby you think, "I'm Buddha; I'm an emanation of the Buddha." You already know that there's no such thing. But with Tantrayana, "My body is a buddha body—as clean clear as crystal, and radiating light; my speech is mantra—whenever I open my mouth, good things manifest; my thought is wisdom." Somehow, you become transcendental; you bring the enlightenment experience into the *now*. That is the beauty of Tantrayana.

From the cultural point of view, when you people look at me, I'm mumbling mantras with this *mala*, I'm wearing these strange clothes; I'm surrounded by strange art and so forth. You get culture shock. And sometimes you're in conflict: "Why do I need these things? Why do we have these things? I don't want this Tibetan trip." And when it comes to mantra: "Why do mantras? I'd be better off saying 'coffee, coffee, coffee, coffee!'"

One way, Tibetan Buddhism says that liberation is an inner thing, but the other way, it has too many external things. But we're not yet buddha; that's why we need help. We need help. Actually, mantra *is* an inner thing. We do mantra in order to develop comprehension. That's a small example. What I'm saying is that to recite mantras, we don't need a rosary. People practicing Tibetan Tantrayana don't need rosaries! It's true. That's what we should understand. But of course, sometimes they can be useful too!

Now I'm a little lost somewhere!

So, by using a skillful method, it's possible for your life to become a transcendental experience. Your life can perhaps become an enlightened experience. Maybe I shouldn't use those words, but I think it can become an enlightened experience.

But you should not be in conflict or get mixed up when in one way you have the Tantrayana recognition that, "I am Chenrezig; I am the Buddha; I am totality," and in another way you again have to do all the relative things [like saying mantras].

Tantrayana is the way to achieve the perfect body, speech and mind we need in order to help other people. The purpose of meditation is not to reach nirvana and then disappear. If that were the case, it would be better that you manifested as a flower. The purpose is to emanate in the beautiful, radiant, white light body of Chenrezig, as clean and as clear as crystal. That emanation can really help people. Sometimes Westerners worry, "I'm practicing meditation so much; perhaps eventually I'll disappear into nothingness. Then what can I do?" Better learn Tantrayana and instead of disappearing, emanate as Avalokiteshvara—transform the purity of your consciousness into the complete, pure body of Avalokiteshvara.

Perhaps I can put it together this way. Each of us *does* have a psychic, or conscious, body as well as a physical body. It is not this blood and bone body that we are radically transforming into Chenrezig. It's not that radically, my body becomes Chenrezig. But my consciousness, or psyche, can transform. Perhaps you can say that one aspect of my psyche is already Chenrezig.

For example, each day of our life we manifest differently. When we get angry, a wrathful manifestation comes out. Sometimes we manifest as Chenrezig, loving kindness, and try to give all of our body, speech and mind to others. You can see; you become an entirely different person. We know this according to our own and each other's lives. Sometimes our dear friend becomes so good, like Chenrezig. And sometimes so wrathful that we get hurt and our heart breaks.

You can see this objectively, if you look at one person; we've all experienced it. We don't know what's happened to this person: "What happened to him?" What makes this change happen? For thirty years the person is one way and then all of a sudden, he's the opposite. We want to understand why it has happened but we don't understand. Of course, I don't understand either.

So, that is the beauty of the human being. Human beings have so many aspects, qualities—good and bad—and different manifestations. If you are sensitive, you can see them through the aura, or vibration—especially Californian people. They always say, "Oh, those are not such good vibrations; oh, very good vibrations." Sometimes it seems that they are very sensitive, but I'm not sure about that. I'm doubtful! I don't know what that is! Maybe that's a new expression. We know people who use that kind of language. But those examples are similar. Tantrayana has reasonable scientific explanations; it's not something imaginary. It relates to the circumstances of our life.

Both Buddhist sutra and tantra say that the nature of the human mind is clean clear light; clean clear mind. So what I'm saying is that the nature of our consciousness has always been clean clear; is clean clear; and will always be clean clear. You don't need to worry about it.

"But we talk about delusions and confusion. What about that?" Delusion is not the character of our consciousness. Clouds are not the character of the sky. You have to change the attitude that thinks like that. Fundamentally, we are wrong when we think, "I am delusion; I'm a bad person who always has bad thoughts; who always acts badly." You cannot sum up your whole, "I am this." It's not true. You cannot put limitations on even your own reality. You cannot; you should not. Each of us has problems and difficulties, but we also have something similar to buddha and bodhisattva energy within us. We do; we do.

For example, sometimes when I'm talking I get surprised at what I'm saying. I don't know what I'm saying. That's a good example, isn't it? I'm an ignorant person, talking like this, and somehow some wisdom also comes out. I can't believe it myself! It's true. I don't think I'm an enlightened being. I don't. But for some reason, good things sometimes come out along with the bad things.

So we should not make limitations when we judge ourselves. Actually, it's like they say in the West: you hear what you want to hear. Exactly like that. When you look within yourself, the quality you want to see appears. If you want to see the bad guy, the bad guy appears; if you want the good guy, the good guy appears. It's true. The thing is not to identify with your delusions. The quality you look for appears.

The example I like to use for the Western mind is that in the world, there are so many men and women. As a matter of fact, everybody is handsome or beautiful. Can you imagine? Somewhere, there's someone who finds you handsome or beautiful. There is; there is. So, that is scientific evidence that we are all handsome; we are all beautiful. Because some mind says you are beautiful—even though you are ugly!

But it functions in that way. When some person sees you as handsome or beautiful, that's exactly the way it works for that person. Let's say I think all of you are beautiful or handsome; for me, that's how you appear; for me, that's reality. But maybe somebody else thinks you're all ugly. I don't care what he thinks; that's his business. What appears to me is my business; that's what affects me. Anyway, you can see that's how reality is.

Look at modern society. Many people put themselves down; that's their worst problem. You can see this everywhere in the world; people put limitations on themselves, on their own reality.

This reality, this judgment of the neurotic ego, is the human problem. Tantra has the methods to eliminate this immediately. So, you become the deity, having the divine pride that you yourself are a buddha, fully complete, and in that way you eliminate the ordinary ego projection.

Also, in this way objects you see don't irritate you. Objects don't irritate you. Now, when you see certain people, you immediately get irritated. That's karma. Something within you is magnetized; it is not out there. You have the preconceived notion, "He looked at me with his eye this way; therefore, I dislike him." You have a preconceived idea. We all do; to some extent, we all do. With certain kinds of people, we're very easygoing, but we're unsure of other people who present themselves in some other way. That is due to preconception; the ego's conception. We should be happy, *really* happy, to connect with any people—even the Shah of Iran, or the Ayatollah! We should be happy.

Take the preconceived idea of the Ayatollah: "This man; this man...." Our ego builds up such energy, can you imagine, that in our next life, when we are children, as soon as we hear the word Ayatollah, we think, "Ayatollah? I don't like." Normally we'd explain it as energy previously built up by the ego, "The Ayatollah is no good." Well, that's the way it happens. It's so easy to say that he's no good, and at the moment you might think that it's not doing any harm, but the thing is that it's not the Ayatollah who harms us, it's the energy that our own ego accumulates that gives us harm.

The reason I'm talking about this topic is that it's difficult for new people to relate to the idea that one can become Chenrezig; it's a new conception. "Who is Chenrezig? Some Chinese man? Some Tibetan man? Who is that? He doesn't exist anywhere in the world. Who's seen him?" Maybe you ask, "Has he seen me? I haven't seen him either." Well, my feeling is that even if we're ugly, our body is not handsome, still, since we were born up to now, an extremely clean clear, organic body has simultaneously existed within us, even while we've had this complicated body. That's the way I feel.

Of course, there are also yoga methods for transforming even this physical body into light. Even this body that our ego has built up in such a heavy, concrete way, "My body is bad," criticizing it as we normally do; "My body is heavy; this and that..." and so forth. So, by practicing, we can make this body light; the difficult heavy one disappears. For some reason, we can do this. Many times we experience symptoms that are simply made by our conceptions. For example, when I was in England last year I met a Tibetan lama who had come from India. He had a problem with his throat; somehow, he felt it was always blocked. When English doctors checked him out, they couldn't find anything physically wrong; it was all in his mind. Incredible, isn't it? Well, that's possible. There's nothing wrong with the body; the only thing that's wrong is the head. I'm sure you can think of many examples of this, where people say, "I hurt here, and here..." but it's only a symptom of a mental problem, not the physical body. I think this definitely happens.

I have more experience of this. I have an English friend whom I

75

met when I was first meeting Western people in India. When he's unhappy, he always gets pain in his hip. He's a very strong guy, but if somebody makes him unhappy, he immediately gets sick there. I'm sure you know people similar to this. This is a good example. It shows that when the sick mind is strong, the body gets sick.

The system of Tantrayana is not something disorderly or something that you have to believe in with blind faith. The Tibetan system is set up dialectically; you can study it philosophically. I'm just talking here; there's no time to study tantra philosophically from beginning to end. But if you want to, you can; it's all there, dialectically, intellectually. The study of tantra can be super-intellectual. That's possible.

However, tantra has four schools; we call them *cha-gyü, chö-gyü, näl-jor-gyü,* and *näl-jor-la-na-me-pa—kriya, charya, yoga,* and *mahayoga,* or *maha-anuttara yoga.* These schools present tantra differently. Like the lam-rim has small, medium and great levels, so too do these four schools—just as those who practice it also have their own level, or degree, of capability. But while all four schools take the energy of desire as the path to enlightenment, there are degrees. *Maha* means great.

Now, as far as receiving initiation is concerned, I don't know much English, but initiation means something like initial experience, or beginning experience. When you receive initiation, you are beginning to get a taste of transformation; there's some communication; transformation is beginning to happen. That is empowerment. But the experience you get at the beginning is in accordance with your own magnetized readiness. Perhaps the first time you receive an empowerment, *pam!*—you immediately get some kind of result. But if you're like me, slow, perhaps nothing happens during your first experience and you need to receive initiation repeatedly in order to generate the kind of nuclear energy that makes an empowerment perfect.

Also, initiations themselves have many levels, or degrees. For example, of the four schools, the kriya and charya have only the first, the vase initiation; they don't have the rest. Furthermore, the first initiation itself also has degrees; you can't have the maha-anuttara yoga vase initiation experience in kriya or charya. But I don't think we need to go into all those details; you're not ready for them yet. Nor is it necessary to bring them up here. However, you should understand that there are degrees of initiation. Also, different deities have different numbers of initiation. For example, Yamantaka has four initiations; Kalachakra has sixteen; and so forth.

However, to some extent, an initiation is for you to receive an experience. It's like planting a seed. This is then repeatedly generated, fertilizing it, until finally it becomes a totally unified realization.

So, in preparation for this, we meditate upon and actualize the three principal aspects of the path. I've told you about these in a simple way, so I don't need to repeat it again. So, you people should be somewhat advanced. Instead of thinking that the lam-rim is so big, it should be a small package for you. In one meditation, when something changes, you should be able to direct your mind into renunciation; another change happens, let it happen—no rejection; no acceptance; let go, let it happen—then put that into bodhicitta meditation. When something else happens, put it into shunyata. But maybe I have to explain how to do this.

Contemplate on the clean clear energy of thought. This signifies shunyata: "This is my picture of shunyata." Why? First of all, your consciousness, or mind, is like a mirror. A mirror is a receptor for any object of form; whatever the color, a mirror receives it. It's the same with our consciousness; it's like a mirror; it can receive all kinds of objects of thought. All kinds of reflections appear in our minds—garbage reflections come; good reflections come. That is beauty; human beings are beautiful. Don't think that human beings are like wood. That's why we should respect human beings. Human beings have discriminating wisdom; they have that capacity. So contemplate on clarity—the clear light nature of mind and thought.

First of all, that clarity is formless. It is not color; it does not have color. Recognize it as space; universal space is empty. So, contemplate. The effect of this meditation, its impact, what happens is that, by having the experience of emptiness, empty space, you eliminate superstition and ego conflict. Having this kind of experience eliminates the ego thoughts that crowd your mind.

From there, you are led to having no thoughts at all; no thought. There is thought, but the crowded, gross level thoughts disappear so that you seem to experience no thought. Sort of, "Where are my thoughts? Where am I?" is what you experience. Of course, this is not exactly a shunyata experience, but it serves as such. I'm not sure about that language—what does "serve" mean?

[Student: instead of.] Yes, it serves; perhaps it's better to say it sublimates—that's better. Something happens; there's an inner transformation. We *have* to go through this; we cannot be arrogant and say, "I want an exact experience of complete shunyata!" It's not going to happen. That's just ego. We have to begin somewhere and work towards that experience. We should be satisfied if even that approximate experience comes.

That's enough for today. Thank you so much.

GLOSSARY

(Skt = Sanskrit; Tib = Tibetan)

Atisha (924-1054). The great Indian master renowned for his practice of bodhicitta who came to Tibet to help revive Buddhism and spent the last seventeen years of his life there. His seminal text, *A Lamp for the Path to Enlightenment*, initiated the steps of the path (*Tib: lam-rim*) tradition found in all schools of Tibetan Buddhism. Founder of the Kadampa school, fore-runner of the Gelug.

bodhicitta (*Skt*). The altruistic determination to reach enlightenment for the sole purpose of enlightening all sentient beings.

bodhisattva (*Skt*). Someone whose spiritual practice is directed towards the achievement of enlightenment for the sake of all sentient beings. One who, with the compassionate motivation of bodhicitta, follows the Mahayana path through ten levels to enlightenment.

buddha (*Skt*). A fully enlightened being. One who has removed all obscurations veiling the mind and has developed all good qualities to perfection. The first of the Three Jewels of Refuge. See also *enlightenment, Shakyamuni Buddha.*

cyclic existence (*Skt: samsara; Tib: khor-wa*). The six realms of conditioned existence, three lower—hell, hungry ghost (*Skt: preta*) and animal—and three upper—human, demigod (*Skt: asura*) and god (*Skt: sura*). It is the beginningless, recurring cycle of death and rebirth under the control of delusion and karma and fraught with suffering. It also refers to the contaminated aggregates of a sentient being.

Dharma (*Skt*). Spiritual teachings, particularly those of Shakya-muni Buddha. Literally, that which holds one back from suffering. The second of the Three Jewels of Refuge.

dualistic view. The ignorant view characteristic of the unenlightened mind in which all things are falsely conceived to have

81

concrete self-existence. To such a view, the appearance of an object is mixed with the false image of its being independent or self-existent, thereby leading to further dualistic views concerning subject and object, self and other, this and that and so forth.

ego-mind. The wrong conception, "I am self-existent." Ignorance of the nature of the mind and self.

eight worldly dharmas. The eight mundane concerns for gain, loss, fame, notoriety, praise, blame, happiness and suffering.

enlightenment (Skt: bodhi). Full awakening; buddhahood. The ultimate goal of Buddhist practice, attained when all limitations have been removed from the mind and one's positive potential has been completely and perfectly realized. It is a state characterized by infinite compassion, wisdom and skill.

four noble truths. The truths of suffering, the origin of suffering, the cessation of suffering and the path to the cessation of suffering; the topic of the first turning of the wheel of Dharma— the first discourse ever given by the Buddha.

Gelug / Kagyu / Sakya / Nyingma. The four main schools of Tibetan Buddhism. Lama Yeshe belonged to the Gelug school.

geshe. A monk who has completed a full monastic education in Buddhist philosophy and debate, passed an examination at the end and been awarded a *geshe* degree.

hallucinate. Lama Yeshe's use does not refer to chemically- or illness-induced hallucinations but to inappropriate projections by the ignorant mind. See *superstition.*

Hinayana (Skt). Literally, Small, or Lesser, Vehicle. It is one of the two general divisions of Buddhism. Hinayana practitioners' motivation for following the Dharma path is principally their intense wish for personal liberation from conditioned existence, or samsara. Two types of Hinayana practitioner are identified: hearers and solitary realizers. Cf. *Mahayana.*

Kadampa. School of Tibetan Buddhism founded in the eleventh century by Atisha and his followers, principally his interpreter, Drom-tön-ba.

kalpa (Skt). Eon. According to Shakyamuni Buddha, longer than the amount of time it would take a cube of solid granite to be worn away by being stroked lightly with a piece of fine silk once every hundred years.

lam-rim (Tib). The graduated path. A presentation of Shakyamuni Buddha's teachings in a form suitable for the step-by-step training of a disciple. The lam-rim was first formulated by the great India teacher Atisha (Dipamkara Shrijnana, 982-1055) when he came to Tibet in 1042. See also *three principal paths.*

Mahayana (Skt). Literally, Great Vehicle. It is one of the two general divisions of Buddhism. Mahayana practitioners' motivation for following the Dharma path is principally their intense wish that all sentient beings be liberated from conditioned existence, or samsara, and attain the full enlightenment of buddhahood. The Mahayana has two divisions, Paramitayana (Sutrayana) and Vajrayana (Tantrayana, Mantrayana). Cf. *Hinayana.*

mind (Skt: citta; Tib: sem). Synonymous with consciousness (*Skt: vijnana; Tib: nam-she*) and sentience (*Skt: manas; Tib: yi*). Defined as that which is "clear and knowing"; a formless entity that has the ability to perceive objects. Mind is divided into six primary consciousnesses and fifty-one mental factors.

Nagarjuna (Skt). The second century A.D. Indian Buddhist philosopher who propounded the Madhyamaka philosophy of emptiness.

Padmasambhava (Tib: Guru Rinpoche). Indian tantric master invited to Tibet by King Trisong Detsen in the eighth century. Founder of the Nyingma school of Tibetan Buddhism.

refuge. The door to the Dharma path. A Buddhist takes refuge in the Three Jewels fearing the sufferings of samsara and having faith that Buddha, Dharma and Sangha have the power to lead him or her out of suffering to happiness, liberation or enlightenment.

Sangha (*Skt*). Spiritual community; the third of the Three Jewels of Refuge. Absolute Sangha are those who have directly realized emptiness; relative Sangha are ordained monks and nuns.

Shakyamuni Buddha (563-483 BC). Fourth of the one thousand founding buddhas of this present world age. Born Siddhartha Gotama, a prince of the Shakya clan in north India, he taught the sutra and tantra paths to liberation and enlightenment; founder of what came to be known as Buddhism. (From the *Skt: buddha*— "fully awake.")

shunyata (*Skt*). Emptiness. The absence of all false ideas about how things exist; specifically, the lack of the apparent independent, self-existence of phenomena.

six perfections (*Skt: paramita*). Charity, morality, patience, enthusiastic perseverance, concentration and wisdom.

superstition (*Tib: nam-tog*). Erroneous belief about reality.

three lower realms. The three realms of greatest suffering in cyclic existence, comprising the animal, hungry ghost (*Skt: preta*) and hell realms.

three principal paths. The three main divisions of the lam-rim: renunciation, bodhicitta and right view.

Tsong Khapa, Lama Je (1357-1417). Founder of the Gelug tradition of Tibetan Buddhism and revitalizer of many sutra and tantra lineages and the monastic tradition in Tibet.

yana (*Skt*). Literally, vehicle. An inner vehicle that carries you along the spiritual path to enlightenment. Buddhism is divided into two main vehicles, *Hinayana* and *Mahayana*.

LAMA YESHE WISDOM ARCHIVE

The LAMA YESHE WISDOM ARCHIVE (LYWA) is the collected works of Lama Thubten Yeshe and Lama Thubten Zopa Rinpoche. The ARCHIVE was founded in 1996 by Lama Zopa Rinpoche, its spiritual director, to make available in various ways the teachings it contains. Distribution of free booklets of edited teachings is one of the ways.

Lama Yeshe and Lama Zopa Rinpoche began teaching at Kopan Monastery, Nepal, in 1970. Since then, their teachings have been recorded and transcribed. At present the LYWA contains more than 7,000 cassette tapes, all of which have now been digitized, and approximately 50,000 pages of transcribed teachings on computer disk. Many tapes, mostly teachings by Lama Zopa Rinpoche, remain to be transcribed. As Rinpoche continues to teach, the number of tapes in the ARCHIVE increases accordingly. Most of the transcripts have been neither checked nor edited.

Here at LYWA we are making every effort to organize the transcription of that which has not yet been transcribed, to edit that which has not yet been edited, and generally to do the many other tasks detailed over. In all this, we need your help. Please contact us for more information:

LAMA YESHE WISDOM ARCHIVE
PO Box 356, Weston, MA 02493, USA
Telephone (781) 899-9587; Fax (413) 845-9239
info@LamaYeshe.com
www.LamaYeshe.com

THE ARCHIVE TRUST

The work of the LAMA YESHE WISDOM ARCHIVE falls into two categories: archiving and dissemination.

ARCHIVING requires managing the audiotapes of teachings by Lama Yeshe and Lama Zopa Rinpoche that have already been collected, collecting recordings of teachings given but not yet sent to the ARCHIVE, and collecting recordings of Lama Zopa's on-going teachings, talks, advice and so forth as he travels the world for the benefit of all. Tapes and disks are then catalogued and stored safely while being kept accessible for further work.

We organize the transcription of tapes, add the transcripts to the already existent database of teachings, manage this database, have transcripts checked, and make transcripts available to editors or others doing research on or practicing these teachings.

Other archiving activities include working with videotapes and photographs of the Lamas and digitizing ARCHIVE materials.

DISSEMINATION involves making the Lamas' teachings available directly or indirectly through various avenues such as booklets for free distribution, regular books for the trade, lightly edited transcripts, floppy disks, audio- and videotapes and CDs, and articles in Mandala and other magazines, and on our Web site. Irrespective of the method we choose, the teachings require a significant amount of work to prepare them for distribution.

This is just a summary of what we do. The ARCHIVE was established with virtually no seed funding and has developed solely through the kindness of many people, some of whom we have mentioned at the front of this book and most of the others on our Web site. We sincerely thank them all.

Our further development similarly depends upon the generosity of those who see the benefit and necessity of this work, and we would be extremely grateful for your help.

THE ARCHIVE TRUST has been established to fund the above activities and we hereby appeal to you for your kind support. If you would like to make a contribution to help us with any of the above tasks or to sponsor booklets for free distribution, please contact us at our Weston address.

The LAMA YESHE WISDOM ARCHIVE is a 501(c)(3) tax-deductible, non-profit corporation (ID number 04-3374479) dedicated to the welfare of all sentient beings and totally dependent upon your donations for its continued existence.

Thank you so much for your support. You may contribute by mailing a check, bank draft or money order to our Weston address; by making a donation on our secure Web site; by mailing or faxing us your credit card number or by phoning it in; or by transferring funds directly to our bank—ask us for details.

THE FOUNDATION FOR THE PRESERVATION OF THE MAHAYANA TRADITION

The Foundation for the Preservation of the Mahayana Tradition (FPMT) is an international organization of Buddhist meditation study and retreat centers, both urban and rural, monasteries, publishing houses, healing centers and other related activities founded in 1975 by Lama Thubten Yeshe and Lama Thubten Zopa Rinpoche. At present, there are more than 150 FPMT activities in over thirty countries worldwide.

The FPMT has been established to facilitate the study and practice of Mahayana Buddhism in general and the Tibetan Gelug tradition, founded in the fifteenth century by the great scholar, yogi and saint, Lama Je Tsong Khapa, in particular.

Every three months, the Foundation publishes a magazine, *Mandala,* from its International Office in the United States of America. To subscribe or view back issues, please go to the *Mandala* Web site, www.mandalamagazine.org, or contact:

FPMT
PO Box 888, Taos, NM 87571, USA
Telephone (505) 758-7766; fax (505) 758-7765
fpmtinfo@fpmt.org
www.fpmt.org

Our Web site also offers teachings by His Holiness the Dalai Lama, Lama Yeshe, Lama Zopa Rinpoche and many other highly respected teachers in the tradition, details about the FPMT's educational programs, audio through FPMT radio, a complete listing of FPMT centers all over the world and in your area, and links to FPMT centers on the Web, where you will find details of their programs, and to other interesting Buddhist and Tibetan home pages.

Lama Zopa Rinpoche
Teachings from the Vajrasattva Retreat

Edited by Ailsa Cameron and Nicholas Ribush

This book is an edited transcript of Rinpoche's teachings during the Vajrasattva retreat at Land of Medicine Buddha, California, February through April, 1999. It contains explanations of the various practices done during the retreat, such as Vajrasattva purification, prostrations to the Thirty-five Buddhas, Lama Chöpa, making light offerings, liberating animals and much, much more. There are also many weekend public lectures covering general topics such as compassion and emptiness. The appendices detail several of the practices taught, for example, the short Vajrasattva sadhana, light offerings, liberating animals and making charity of water to Dzambhala and the pretas.

It is essential reading for all Lama Zopa Rinpoche's students, especially retreat leaders and FPMT center spiritual program coordinators, and serious Dharma students everywhere.

704 pp., detailed table of contents, 7 appendices
6" x 9" paperback
ISBN 1-891868-04-7
US$20 & shipping and handling

Available from the LYWA, Wisdom Publications (Boston), Wisdom Books (London), Mandala Books (Melbourne), Snow Lion Publications (USA) and FPMT centers everywhere. Discount for bookstores. Free for members of the International Mahayana Institute.

OTHER TEACHINGS OF
LAMA YESHE AND LAMA ZOPA RINPOCHE
CURRENTLY AVAILABLE

BOOKS PUBLISHED BY WISDOM PUBLICATIONS

Wisdom Energy, by Lama Yeshe and Lama Zopa Rinpoche
Introduction to Tantra, by Lama Yeshe
Transforming Problems, by Lama Zopa Rinpoche
The Door to Satisfaction, by Lama Zopa Rinpoche
The Tantric Path of Purification, by Lama Yeshe
The Bliss of Inner Fire, by Lama Yeshe
Becoming the Compassion Buddha, by Lama Yeshe

You may see more information about and order the above titles at the Wisdom Web site, www.wisdompubs.org, or call toll free in the USA on 1-800-272-4050.

TRANSCRIPTS

Several transcripts of teachings by Lama Yeshe and Lama Zopa Rinpoche are also available. See the Lama Yeshe Wisdom Archive Web site for more details.

VIDEOS OF LAMA YESHE

We are in the process of converting our VHS videos of Lama Yeshe's teachings to CD. See opposite for more information.

VIDEOS OF LAMA ZOPA RINPOCHE

See the FPMT Web site for more information. You will also find there many recommended practices written or compiled by Rinpoche.

THE TEACHINGS IN THIS BOOK ARE AVAILABLE ON VIDEO

Now you can see and hear Lama Yeshe giving them.

We no longer have the actual videotapes available, but they have been digitized and put onto CDs that play in Real Audio on your computer. We also plan to make them into DVDs before too long. Stay in touch or watch our Web site to find out more.

Three Principal Aspects of the Path

During His Holiness the Dalai Lama's 1982 teachings at Institut Vajra Yogini, France, Lama Yeshe was asked to "baby-sit" the audience for a couple of days when His Holiness manifested illness. The result is this excellent two-part introduction to the path to enlightenment, in which Lama explains renunciation, bodhicitta and the right view of emptiness.

Introduction to Tantra

In 1980, in California, Lama Yeshe gave a commentary to the Avalokiteshvara (Chenrezig) yoga method. These two tapes are Lama's introduction to this series (*the other six tapes are waiting for funds so that we can finish preparing them...please help!*) and constitute a wonderful explanation of the fundamentals of tantric practice.

These CDs are free. All we ask is that you pay for the shipping. See our Web site for more information: www.LamaYeshe.com.

DISCOVERING BUDDHISM AT HOME
Awakening the limitless potential of your mind,
achieving all peace and happiness

This program is designed as an experiential course in Tibetan Buddhist philosophy and practice. The teachings contained herein are drawn from the Geluk tradition of Lama Tsong Khapa, a great saint and scholar of the 14th century. These teachings come in an unbroken lineage from Shakyamuni Buddha, who first imparted them over 2,500 years ago, since when they have passed directly from teacher to disciple down to this present day.

The realizations of Shakyamuni Buddha cannot be measured, but it is said that the Buddha gained direct insight into the nature of reality, perfected the qualities of wisdom, compassion and power, and then revealed the path to accomplish those same realizations to his disciples. The Buddha's teachings have been presented in various ways by different holy beings over the centuries to make them more accessible to those of us who did not have the opportunity to meet the Buddha ourselves. Lama Tsong Khapa was one such holy being and his teachings of the "lam-rim" or "graduated path to enlightenment" form the core of the Discovering Buddhism at Home program.

In addition, two contemporary masters, Lama Thubten Yeshe (1935-1984), and Lama Zopa Rinpoche (1945-present), have imparted these teachings to their students in a deep and experiential way, leading thousands of seekers to discover for themselves the truth of what the Buddha taught. The methods and teachings found in this program also reflect the unique styles of these two great teachers and are meant to help students get an experiential taste of the Buddha's words.

There are two levels of participation that you may choose from when you embark on this program. Within each module there are discourses, meditations and other practices, readings and assessment questions listed. As a casual student you may do some or all of the above as per your wish. Alternatively, you can engage in this program as a certificate student. In this case you will see on the summary sheet that comes with each module what requirements are to be fulfilled. With each module you will also receive a "Completion Card," which is to be filled out by any Discovering Buddhism at Home student who chooses to get a certificate. When all 14 cards have been completed you will receive a certificate of completion. This can be done at any time and the cards do not need to be filled out in order. This certificate simply awards one the satisfaction of having completed a very comprehensive engagement with the path to enlightenment.

Discovering Buddhism at Home is intended to be more than an academic undertaking. As such, those who wish to gain some experience of what the Buddha taught are encouraged to make it a personal goal to fulfill all of these requirements and thus receive a final completion certificate issued by the Education Department of FPMT and FPMT's Spiritual Director, Lama Zopa Rinpoche. Your completion certificate is symbolic of your commitment to spiritual awakening and you should rejoice deeply when you receive it, let alone be moved by how your mind has changed in the process!

The Discovering Buddhism at Home package includes the following:

A different Western teacher teaches each module. You will receive these teachings on audio CD (the length of each module varies but there are approximately 4-8 teaching CDs per module). Additionally, you will receive audio CDs of the guided meditations (2-4 CDs per module) and a text CD entitled "Course Materials" containing the written transcripts of the teachings.

Each module also has a "Course Materials" text CD that contains all the written transcripts of the teachings and meditations in printed form as well as a text CD with all of the Discovering Buddhism Required Reading materials for all 14 modules of the program. (Please Note: the Text CD does not include the published texts, which are one's own responsibility to acquire. Please see "Required and Suggested Reading" for a full listing of these.)

A chat room has been created exclusively for Discovering Buddhism at Home participants. When you purchase a DB module you will receive instructions on how to become a member of the chat room. This feature gives students the opportunity to enhance their learning experience through virtual discussion groups.

The cost is $50–60 per module and we expect that it will take you approximately two months to complete each one, if you fulfill all the requirements. However, you are free to buy the modules in a time frame that suits you, i.e., when you finish one you simply buy the next. Students who wish to receive a completion certificate will also receive the support of an FPMT elder, who will reply to your answers to the assessment questions. This is to ensure that you are on track with your understanding and to help give you guidance as you progress through the 14 modules.

We will have a new module ready for distribution very 8 weeks throughout 2003 and 2004. These modules can be purchased directly from the FPMT shop at www.fpmt.org/shop or by writing to: materials@fpmt.org.

Regardless of the level of participation you choose to make in this program, we pray that you will enjoy the time you spend Discovering Buddhism at Home and that it brings you all happiness, both temporal and ultimate. For more information, please refer to the Web page: www.fpmt.org/dbhome/default.asp.

With prayers for your success,
FPMT Education Department Staff

WHAT TO DO WITH DHARMA TEACHINGS

The Buddhadharma is the true source of happiness for all sentient beings. Books like the one in your hand show you how to put the teachings into practice and integrate them into your life, whereby you get the happiness you seek. Therefore, anything containing Dharma teachings or the names of your teachers is more precious than other material objects and should be treated with respect. To avoid creating the karma of not meeting the Dharma again in future lives, please do not put books (or other holy objects) on the floor or underneath other stuff, step over or sit upon them, or use them for mundane purposes such as propping up wobbly tables. They should be kept in a clean, high place, separate from worldly writings, and wrapped in cloth when being carried around. These are but a few considerations.

Should you need to get rid of Dharma materials, they should not be thrown in the rubbish but burned in a special way. Briefly: do not incinerate such materials with other trash, but alone, and as they burn, recite the mantra OM AH HUM. As the smoke rises, visualize that it pervades all of space, carrying the essence of the Dharma to all sentient beings in the six samsaric realms, purifying their minds, alleviating their suffering, and bringing them all happiness, up to and including enlightenment. Some people might find this practice a bit unusual, but it is given according to tradition. Thank you very much.

DEDICATION

Through the merit created by preparing, reading, thinking about and sharing this book with others, may all teachers of the Dharma live long and healthy lives, may the Dharma spread throughout the infinite reaches of space, and may all sentient beings quickly attain enlightenment.

In whichever realm, country, area or place this book may be, may there be no war, drought, famine, disease, injury, disharmony or unhappiness, may there be only great prosperity, may every thing needed be easily obtained, and may all be guided by only perfectly qualified Dharma teachers, enjoy the happiness of Dharma, have only love and compassion for all beings, and only benefit and never harm each other.

LAMA THUBTEN YESHE was born in Tibet in 1935. At the age of six, he entered the great Sera Monastic University, Lhasa, where he studied until 1959, when the Chinese invasion of Tibet forced him into exile in India. Lama Yeshe continued to study and meditate in India until 1967, when, with his chief disciple, Lama Thubten Zopa Rinpoche, he went to Nepal. Two years later he established Kopan Monastery, near Kathmandu, in order to teach Buddhism to Westerners. In 1974, the Lamas began making annual teaching tours to the West, and as a result of these travels a worldwide network of Buddhist teaching and meditation centers—the Foundation for the Preservation of the Mahayana Tradition—began to develop. In 1984, after an intense decade of imparting a wide variety of incredible teachings and establishing one FPMT activity after another, at the age of forty-nine, Lama Yeshe passed away. He was reborn as Osel Hita Torres in Spain in 1985, recognized as the incarnation of Lama Yeshe by His Holiness the Dalai Lama in 1986, and, as the monk Lama Tenzin Osel Rinpoche, is studying for his *geshe* degree at the reconstituted Sera Monastery in South India. Lama's remarkable story is told in Vicki Mackenzie's book, *Reincarnation: The Boy Lama* (Wisdom Publications, 1996).

Some of Lama Yeshe's teachings have also been published by Wisdom. Books include *Wisdom Energy; Introduction to Tantra; The Tantric Path of Purification; The Bliss of Inner Fire* and *Becoming the Compassion Buddha.* Transcripts in print are *Light of Dharma; Life, Death and After Death;* and *Transference of Consciousness at the Time of Death.* Available through FPMT centers or at www.wisdompubs.org. Other teachings may be found on line at www.LamaYeshe.com.

Lama Yeshe on video: *Introduction to Tantra* and *The Three Principal Aspects of the Path.* See the detailed information in this book. Available from the LAMA YESHE WISDOM ARCHIVE.

DR. NICHOLAS RIBUSH, MB, BS, is a graduate of Melbourne University Medical School (1964) who first encountered Buddhism at Kopan Monastery, Nepal, in 1972. Since then he has been a student of Lama Yeshe and Lama Zopa Rinpoche and a full time worker for their international organization, the Foundation for the Preservation of the Mahayana Tradition (FPMT). He was a monk from 1974 to 1986. He established FPMT archiving and publishing activities at Kopan in 1973, and with Lama Yeshe founded Wisdom Publications in 1975. Between 1981 and 1996 he served variously as Wisdom's director, editorial director and director of development. Over the years he has edited and published many teachings by Lama Yeshe and Lama Zopa Rinpoche, and established and/or directed several other FPMT activities, including the International Mahayana Institute, Tushita Mahayana Meditation Centre, the Enlightened Experience Celebration, Mahayana Publications, Kurukulla Center for Tibetan Buddhist Studies and now the LAMA YESHE WISDOM ARCHIVE. He was a member of the FPMT board of directors from its inception in 1983 until 2002.